Contents

Preface

This book is intended for students on a wide variety of business studies and other courses who wish to learn about databases, as well as for students in adult education classes. Undergraduate students on computing courses may also find the book a very useful supplement to more theoretical texts on database design.

In my experience, students find it more difficult to become productive with database software than other products such as word processors. In part, this is because the concepts of document processing are already known (most people know how to put together a letter), whereas the structure of a database can seem completely alien. In addition, many students find existing texts about database design overly theoretical.

The reason for this theoretical bias is largely historical. Many early texts about relational databases were intended more as polemics than explanations – when the relational model was first propounded it was promoted as being mathematically correct, so early texts concentrated on mathematical 'proofs' (as well as using a great deal of jargon). Subsequent texts have often followed this model.

This book promotes a practical approach to the design and management of databases. Units 1 to 7 cover the design process prior to creating a database. This process can be followed irrespective of the database product being used. Units 8 to 17 go on to show how the concepts explained in the first part are implemented using Microsoft Access™.

The book assumes no previous experience of databases or any other database package. The sections on implementing the design using Microsoft Access assume some familiarity with the Windows 95™ operating system.

This book does not attempt to provide complete coverage of the Microsoft Access product. For a task-oriented approach to learning more about Microsoft Access, the reader is directed to Access 7 Further Skills by S Coles and J Rowley, also published by Letts Educational.

Nick Dowling

1998

Database Design
& Management

using Access

Nick Dowling

 continuum
LONDON • NEW YORK

Acknowledgments

A number of people have been involved in the production of this
book. I would like to thank Ed Peppitt who commissioned the
book prior to his leaving Letts, Nathalie Manners who carried the
project forward, and Tanya Solomons who organised the
production and kept everything on track.
I would also like to thank my colleagues John Brewster and
Ed Swinfen who reviewed the manuscript and made useful
suggestions for improvements.

Finally, I would like to thank my wife Janet and children Carmen
and Aaron for their love and support, and for putting up with me
spending so much time in front of the computer.

Access ™ Screen Shots © Microsoft Corporation.

Reprinted by permission from Microsoft Corporation.

Oracle is a registered trademark of Oracle Corporation.

£10.99

A CIP record for this book is available from the British Library.

ISBN 0 8264 5390 2

Project management: Tanya Solomons

Typeset by Barbara Linton and Tessa Barwick

Printed in Great Britain Martins the Printers, Berwick upon Tweed
Continuum
The Tower Building, 11 York Road, London, SE1 7NX
370 Lexington Avenue, New York, NY 10017-6550

1 Introduction

What you will learn in this unit

This unit introduces you to the key concepts of information processing. In order to put these concepts into context, the unit provides a brief historical overview of record keeping. It then provides definitions for a number of key terms, and goes on to discuss why information has become so important to our society in this century.

At the end of this unit you should:

❏ understand that the need to maintain records has existed throughout history

❏ appreciate that the ability to store and process information has been fundamentally changed by the introduction of information technology

❏ understand the difference between data and information, and be able to describe the methods by which data can be transformed into information

❏ be able to describe the characteristics of quality information

❏ be able to provide a definition of a database and of a Database Management System

❏ be able to give examples of how databases are used in the real world

❏ understand the different types of database systems used in organisations.

Keeping records

Mankind has been keeping records since the dawn of civilisation. The oldest surviving examples of records made by humans are purely pictorial in form. Paintings of animals dating back more than 15,000 years ago have been found in caves in Spain and France. As civilisations developed, pictorial records changed into pictographic representations (such as the hieroglyphics used by the Egyptians) and then into the alphabetic systems we use today. At the same time, the change from subsistence economies to ones based on trade necessitated the recording of numerical and financial information as well as records of people and events.

From very early this kind of quantitative information was kept in lists. Lists of items can be found in the hieroglyphics on many buildings in Egyptian archaeological sites. Later these lists took on a more structured form with the arrangement of rows and columns which we now call a ledger. Until the twentieth century almost all of these records were maintained by hand, usually on paper. At the turn of the twentieth century financial institutions employed dozens of clerks whose sole purpose was to maintain these handwritten records.

The computer has changed all this. Instead of keeping records on paper, almost every major organisation now keeps its records in electronic form and processes them using a computer system. As a result, the army of clerks is no longer required. Therefore the introduction of the computer has led to major changes in employment patterns throughout the western world.

Throughout the twentieth century there has been a shift in employment patterns away from primary industries such as agriculture and manufacturing to service industries, and there is no sign of this trend being reversed. During the second half of the twentieth century this trend has been accelerated by the increasing use of information technology (computers and electronic communications). At the heart of the majority of these computerised information-processing systems you will find a database.

The Information Age

Today we live in an information age and the societies of Western Europe, North America, Japan and Australasia have been described as information societies. An information society can be characterised as one in which a greater part of the working population is involved in service industries such as finance and insurance, administration, education, the media and so on. Individuals employed in these service industries are often called knowledge workers. Instead of producing food, raw materials or finished goods, these workers work with information to provide a service.

Information as an organisational resource

The well-being of individuals, organisations and even nations can depend upon access to quality information. For many organisations, the information that they have at their disposal has come to be seen as one of its main resources (along with the staff that they employ and the technology that they use). Organisations may depend on information in many ways:

- in order to make the best purchasing choice, it is necessary to know where the item you wish to purchase is available and which of these outlets is offering the best price

- in order to make the best decision regarding the launch of a new product, an organisation should have an understanding of its customer base and the market for the product

- in order to make the best decision regarding its defence, a nation must have accurate information about the capabilities and intentions of other nations (such information is commonly called intelligence).

However it is not the case that the organisation that has the most information will make the best decisions. The term 'information overload' is used to describe a situation where there is too much information to be useful. In fact the term 'data overload' might be more appropriate to describe this situation, because there is a fundamental difference between data and information.

What is data?

DEFINITION

Data can be defined as individual facts about something or somebody that have not been organised (sometimes called 'raw data'). A random collection of names and telephone numbers is just data.

What is information?

DEFINITION

Information can be defined as data that has been organised in such a way as to be useful to somebody. A telephone directory contains information because it has been organised (by sorting the names into alphabetical order) to enable you to find the telephone number for an individual or organisation.

You can see from this definition that what may be considered useful information to one person in a particular circumstance may be considered as simply data to another person in another circumstance.

When data is organised and converted into information by a computer system it is called processing. There are a number of ways that data can be processed.

Sorting – the data can be reordered so that it is easier to find or compare data items.

Searching – an individual data item can be found from the hundreds, thousands, or even millions of other data items.

Filtering – a smaller set of data items can be selected so that it easier to find the required information.

Aggregating – items can be grouped, added together, counted and so on to produce a summary of the data.

Performing additional calculations – new values can be calculated from the data items that exist.

Sources of data

Organisations can obtain data from a number of different sources.

From elsewhere in the organisation. It is an increasing trend for organisations to analyse the data that they already possess to obtain new insights from the information that it provides. For example, data from the orders placed by customers can provide useful information to a marketing department. However, it is often the case that data in existing systems is not useful because it is not readily accessible or it is in the wrong format.

From publicly available sources. Data can be obtained from publicly available sources such as a library, or from the Internet.

From their customers or suppliers. Organisations can obtain information about their customers or suppliers by asking them to complete surveys, or other marketing techniques. In recent years retailers have introduced loyalty cards, one function of which is to obtain marketing information regarding customers.

From commercial sources. Organisations can buy data such as mailing lists from a commercial source.

Characteristics of useful information

If information is defined as data that has been organised in such a way as to be useful to somebody, how do we define what is useful? In some ways it is easier to recognise useless information, rather than useful information. Useful information should have the following characteristics.

Up to date – correct decisions can only be made if information is up to date. For example, a decision regarding restocking will only be correct if the information about current inventory levels is up to date. If it is out of date, it is useless.

On time – information needs to be timely. If a restocking order has to be placed by a certain deadline, information about inventory levels will only be useful if it is received before that deadline. If it is received too late, it is useless.

Relevant – information is useful only if it is relevant to the task at hand. For example, information regarding employees' remuneration levels is not directly relevant to a decision regarding inventory levels used for stock control.

Complete – a decision to reorder any items will only be correct if the information about inventory levels includes the quantity held in stock at all possible locations.

Consistent – it is not possible to make the correct decision if information is contradictory. This can happen if the data is duplicated in different locations and each location has not been updated consistently. This can also happen if the same data is processed differently, leading to inconsistent results.

Presented in useable form – information can be useless if it shows too much detail and requires additional processing or analysis.

Accessible to authorised personnel – information may be available within an organisation, but individuals will only be able to make the correct decisions if they are able to get access to it. If the purchasing department does not have access to inventory levels, it is likely that they will make uninformed decisions.

Secured against unauthorised access – information that is not secured against unauthorised access may be changed or deleted either inadvertently or maliciously. If this happens (or is thought to have happened) the information cannot be relied upon.

Information processing

Data is transformed into information in a computer system by processing. There are four key aspects of information processing.

1. Capturing data

The process of data capture is often called input, and the parts of the computer that do this work are called input devices.

Before information can be produced by a computer system the raw data must be captured. Data can be captured in computer systems by a number of means:

- entering data into the computer using the keyboard and/or mouse of a personal computer (PC) or visual display unit (VDU)
- scanning information into the computer from barcodes, or other machine-readable coding systems
- transferring data in electronic form from one computer system to another.

2. Storing data

The parts of the computer used to store large amounts of data are often referred to as mass storage devices.

Once data has been captured it can be processed immediately then discarded. More often the data will be stored for later use on devices such as a hard disk, a computer tape archive, or on a CD-ROM.

3. Processing data

This is the actual manipulation of the data by sorting, searching, filtering, aggregation or calculation to become information. The part of a computer that performs all the processing is called the central processing unit (CPU).

4. Communicating information

After processing, the information must be communicated in a useable form. Information can be presented:

- temporarily on the screen of a PC or VDU

- on paper by using a printer or plotter

- in other formats such as microfiche.

What is a database?

The combination of software and data that are used to perform these four key aspects of information processing are frequently called databases. However, computers are not the only means of storing data and producing information. Data can be stored in paper ledgers or in card systems, and information can be produced from these sources by analysing the data manually. We can define a database as the following:

DEFINITION

An integrated collection of data organised to meet the needs of one or more users.

Although there are a number of means of creating a database, computers offer great advantages over other means.

- A computerised database can have an almost limitless capacity to store data. Physical storage space is often a limitation of manual methods.

- If designed correctly, a computerised database can enable data to be reorganised in many different ways. In contrast, manual systems are organised in one particular way. For example, the telephone directory helps you find a telephone number from a name, but is useless for finding a name from a telephone number. A card system may be organised by name, but imagine the work involved in trying to re-organise the cards by postcode!

- Many people can access computers at the same time. By contrast, if you have removed a card from a card system nobody else can use it.

Examples of uses of a database

We come into contact with computerised databases almost every day of our lives. Examples of uses for computerised databases that we may come into contact with outside of work include:

- banking systems that keep information about customers and their accounts

- point of sales systems in shops that process the purchase of goods

- inventory systems ranging from the books held in a library to the stock held in a furniture shop or car showroom

- reservation systems for booking airline flights and other travel, seats at the theatre or cinema, etc

- licensing systems such as for drivers and vehicles, dog licences or television licenses.

Examples of uses of computerised databases that we may have to use in a working environment include:

- human resources or personnel systems that hold employee information

- payroll systems that process salaries and benefits

- manufacturing systems – many products are now produced by machines that are computer-controlled

- accounting systems that produce invoices, statements and other company accounts.

Database Management Systems

Any system that stores and processes data can be described as a database. Over the last 20 years a number of companies have developed software products that are specifically designed to store and process large amounts of data. These software products are generally known as Database Management Systems (DBMS). A Database Management System can be defined as follows.

DEFINITION

Computer software with the capability to store data in an integrated, structured format and to enable users to retrieve, manipulate and manage the data.

There are many different types of Database Management System, and even more DBMS products on the market. This book discusses the concepts and practice of database design and implementation using one of the most popular DBMS products for the PC – Microsoft Access.

The tools that Microsoft Access provides for information processing

Each of these tools will be described in greater detail later in the book.

Like most DBMS designed for use on PCs, Microsoft Access provides many different tools to enable data to be captured, stored and processed and for the presentation of information. The following sections examine the various tools that Access provides in the context of these key activities of information processing.

Tables for data storage

In most DBMS the data is stored in tables and is presented to the user as an arrangement of rows and columns. Each row contains the data relating to one particular data item (such as a customer) and each column holds data relating to one particular attribute of the data (such as a postcode).

Access displays the data on screen as a table or grid that behaves in a similar way to a spreadsheet. If you already have experience with a spreadsheet product such as Microsoft Excel™, you will find it easy to work with tables in Access.

Data in a table displayed in a data sheet

Data sheet is an arrangement of rows and columns

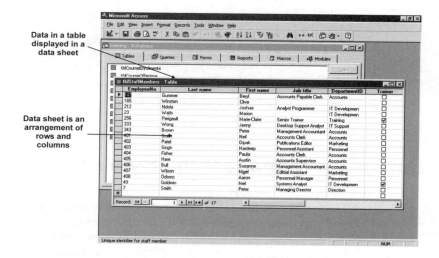

Fig 1.1
Access stores data in tables which can then be viewed as a datasheet

This concept of separating the logical view of the data from the physical storage method is called data independence.

When you are using a DBMS it is not necessary to know anything about the way that the data is physically stored on the particular mass storage device (usually a disk drive) being used. The DBMS handles all the reading and writing of data to and from the disk for you.

Queries, macros and programs for data processing

While tables are used to store the data, they only provide very limited capabilities to process data. Access provides queries, macros and a complete programming language to handle the processing requirements of almost any application.

Queries are very powerful tools that can be used to convert the raw data held in a table into information. Using a query you can change the order of records (sorting), retrieve individual records or groups of records (searching and filtering), count, sum, average and otherwise summarise data values (aggregation) and compute new values from values held in the table (calculation). Queries also allow you to work with data from more than one table at the same time.

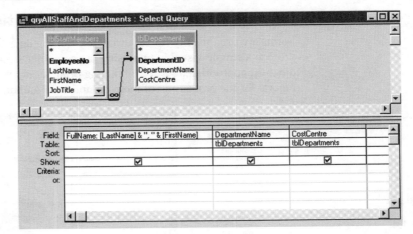

Fig 1.2
Queries allow you to sort, search and filter the data that is held in one or more tables

The result of a query is presented in exactly the same way as a table – as rows and columns. Because of this, you can think of the results of queries as temporary, computed tables.

Access also provides facilities for automating complex or repetitive tasks and for performing more complicated data manipulation and processing using macros and programs written in Visual Basic programming language. However, these advanced features are beyond the scope of this book.

Forms for data capture

It is possible to enter data directly into a table, and users who are used to working with spreadsheets may find this useful. However, there are some kinds of data (such as pictures) that Access cannot display in a table grid.

Additionally, many users are more accustomed to working with one record at a time with the display occupying the whole screen. Access provides

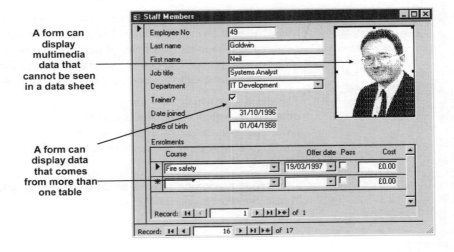

A form can display multimedia data that cannot be seen in a data sheet

A form can display data that comes from more than one table

Fig 1.3
Forms are used for capturing and presenting data on the computer's display screen

Reports for communicating information

Forms are used mainly for capturing and editing data. They can be used to provide a simple visual output using the computer's screen, but they are not the most appropriate tool for producing printed output. Access provides reports for the production of more complicated output.

Although reports are primarily designed for printed output, they can be displayed on screen

A report can display information in both text and graphical format

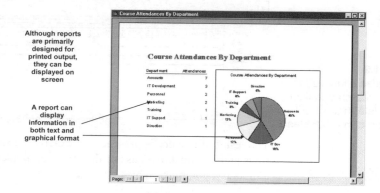

Fig 1.4
Reports are used for presenting information in different formats

Reports can be previewed on screen before printing. The on-screen appearance should be a very close match to the way the report will appear when printed. Reports can contain graphics such as pictures and graphs.

Types of databases

A database can be used to store and process all sorts of data. However, in a business environment you will find that there are two basic types of database, with lots of variations within these two categories.

Transaction processing databases

It is often the case that when transaction processing systems fail an organisation is not able to conduct its business effectively.

Transaction processing databases are used to support the daily business transactions of an organisation and allow each individual transaction to be captured as it happens. Examples of transaction processing database systems include order processing, point of sales systems and banking systems such as the terminals used by tellers and Automatic Teller Machines (ATMs).

The speed with which these transactions can be processed is of paramount importance – often a customer is waiting while the transaction is being processed. With larger systems a vast number of transactions have to be processed almost simultaneously, so volume of throughput is also very important.

Transaction processing systems are also sometimes called On-Line Transaction Processing (OLTP) systems.

Decision support databases

Very large database systems are often called Data Warehouses.

Decision support databases usually contain summaries, subsets or aggregations of the data that is acquired using transaction processing databases. They may also contain data acquired from external sources. Examples of this include data on competitors or data supplied by industry groups or trade associations.

Decision support databases are often required to store huge amounts of historical data. The main purpose of decision support databases is to store the data so that it can be analysed to reveal trends or supply statistical information. This information may be used by management for planning and control or by senior management for strategic planning.

The ability to perform ad hoc queries and to analyse the data from a number of different viewpoints is important in decision support databases. Decision support systems against which ad hoc queries can be made as required are sometimes called On-Line Analytical Processing (OLAP) systems.

Introduction to the case study

In order to demonstrate the concepts that are discussed and to provide meaningful examples of the practical aspects of database design, a single case study is presented throughout the book. The case study has been chosen to be simple enough to demonstrate concepts without getting lost in excessive detail, while sufficiently complex to be able to demonstrate that database design is a constant process of making decisions that involve choices and trade-offs.

Castellan Ltd is a large insurance company based in the South East of England. The training department within Castellan runs internal training courses that cover subjects such as employee induction, fire evacuation procedures, health and safety, as well as training in the bespoke computer systems used within the company. In addition, the department is responsible for advising employees on external training courses that are available for general software packages (such as Microsoft Office) and for coordinating the bookings for these external courses.

Up to now the department has kept its records in a list in an Excel spreadsheet. However, the needs of the department have outgrown what can be achieved in Excel. The decision has been made to analyse the requirements for a new system to meet the information processing needs of the department. Once the requirements are fully understood, a decision will be made whether to buy a ready-made system to meet the requirements (if one exists) or to develop a new bespoke system.

Revision exercises

1. Think of the various places where you have come into contact with a computerised database during the last week. Examples may include borrowing books from a library or taking money from an ATM. How would the activity involved have been different if a manual system had been used instead of a computer?

2. (a) Give examples of the databases that may be used by the staff of a college or university.

   (b) Classify each system as either transaction processing or decision support (or both).

   (c) Give examples of internal and external sources of data for these systems.

3. Give an example of a report that may be considered as useful information by one person, but simply as data by another.

4. Consider the process of selecting a course at a college or university. What information do you require to make the best decision? How do you use this information during the process of making the decision?

2 Beginning the design process

What you will learn in this unit

This unit provides an introduction to the subject of database design. At the end of this unit you should:

- ❏ understand that there are a number of problems that can arise from a poorly designed database

- ❏ understand that when converting an existing computerised system it is unlikely that using the current data structures will lead to the best design

- ❏ understand that a systematic approach to database design is most likely to lead to the implementation of a quality system

- ❏ understand why it is important to set clear goals before embarking on a project to produce a new information system.

Where do databases come from?

The term downsizing has been coined to describe the process of moving systems from mainframe systems to smaller mini-computers, or from mini-computers to stand-alone PCs or a PC network. Upsizing refers to the opposite process of moving PC-based systems to a network server or mini-computer.

The need to create a new database may arise from a number of sources. There may be an existing manual system that has reached the limits of its usefulness and it may be felt that the benefits of using a computerised system will exceed the costs of acquiring, constructing and running the system. These days, however, the number of organisations that continue to use manual systems grows smaller and smaller. More frequently database projects arise from the need to convert or upgrade existing computerised systems.

In some cases these systems may be legacy applications written in programming languages like COBOL. More often the system to be converted to a database application may be as simple as a list maintained by an individual or a department using a spreadsheet program such as Microsoft Excel or a multi-purpose product such as Microsoft Works. The need to move to a database arises because the processing requirements of the organisation may have proved to be beyond the capabilities of this type of product.

Why is database design important?

When converting existing systems it is unlikely that the file structures used in the current system would prove to be the most appropriate in a database solution. Just as the simple automation of an existing manual process will rarely lead to the best solution, simply converting existing file structures to the particular database product being used will not yield the best results.

There are a number of problems that can occur when a database is poorly designed. Fortunately there are well-defined techniques that can be used to avoid these problems. The following section looks at the Excel spreadsheet currently used by Castellan Ltd to store its course information, and discusses the problems that have arisen from the way it has been designed.

The course information system as a single list

The most important requirement for a course information system is the need to keep a record of the staff members who attend each course. The training department in Castellan uses a list on an Excel worksheet to do this.

In a product such as Microsoft Excel the list data is organised as a simple arrangement of rows and columns. Usually all the data is held in a single list or table, even though it may be better to break it up into separate lists. This is because the only way to produce a 'cross-reference' between two separate lists is to use (often complicated) formulas. Excel is not alone in having this problem. Older file processing systems also lack the ability to hold cross-references between files outside of the programs that use them. As these systems do not provide the ability to automatically cross-reference other data they are often called flat files.

The Excel file used by Castellan looks like this:

Course number	Course title	Start date	Attendee1 name	Attendee1 dept	Attendee2 name	Attendee2 dept
IND1	Staff induction	27/03/1998	Neil Smith	Accounts	Dipak Patel	Marketing
FIR1	Fire safety	29/03/1998	Peter Brown	Accounts	Joshua Ndola	IT
ACC1	Introduction to Microsoft Access	24/04/1998	Jenny Wong	Desktop Services	Peter Brown	Accounts
IND1	Staff induction	15/04/1998	Hardeep Singh	Personnel	Paula Fisher	Accounts

Table 2.1 The Excel file used by Castellan to store staff attendance on courses

The columns headed Attendee1 name and Attendee1 dept are repeated enough times to provide sufficient space for the maximum number of staff members who may attend a course at any one time.

Problems with this approach

By examining the data values held in this very simple example we can see some of the problems that result from this approach.

Redundant data

- Each time that a staff member attends a course it is necessary to record their department. This redundancy could be avoided if information about the staff member could be held in a separate list that could be cross-referenced.

- Each row contains a code for the course as well as its title. This redundancy could be avoided if information about the course could be held in a separate list that could be cross-referenced.

Please note that redundant data should not be confused with duplicate values. Where the same fact has to be recorded about different people or things, the database will need to hold the same value more than once. The problem here is the fact that the same data is duplicated unnecessarily.

Inconsistent data

- Looking at the data we can see that Peter Brown has attended two different courses. Each time his department has been recorded differently. It is possible that he has moved from one department to another, in which case you could assume that the most recent record was correct. It is also possible, however, that one of the entries is a typographical error. But which one?

Inflexibility

- With this arrangement of data it is necessary to impose arbitrary limits on its users. For example, at the time that the system was designed the training room at Castellan could only accommodate six people and so the system was designed with this limitation in mind. However, if the company gets another, larger, training room it will be necessary to redesign the list to cope with this. In a spreadsheet this is not too difficult, but in older, file-based systems it can be very difficult indeed.

- Each row in the list has enough fields to hold data about the maximum number of staff members that can attend a course, even if the course was run for only one employee. This leads to a lot of empty columns that take up space on the computer's disk and this is a waste of storage space.

- The ways that you can analyse the data in this example are limited by its design. For example, it would be difficult to find out how many times a particular employee has been on a course as you would have to search in each of the Attendee fields. It would be just as difficult to calculate the average number of attendances on each course.

Limited sharing of data

- When using a spreadsheet the file is manipulated as a single unit. As a result it is not possible for more than one user to update the data in the same file at the same time. One way round this would be for users to have their own copies of the file. However, this usually leads to multiple copies of the same file, each with a different version of the data, taking up lots of space on people's hard disks.

No inherent control of data quality

- In flat file systems such as an Excel list it is necessary to write logic into an application to ensure the quality of the data. In a spreadsheet this could be achieved by an arrangement of formulas and macros, in other systems this type of data validation would be written in the application programming language. Such application logic may have to be rewritten every time the design of the file is changed.

Changing data can lead to unexpected results

This kind of problem is known as an 'update anomaly'.

- If any staff member changes department every occurrence of that staff member would need to be updated to reflect the new data. If one item were missed, it would leave the data in an inconsistent state.

This kind of problem is known as an 'insertion anomaly'.

- The database only holds information about departments if they have sent at least one staff member on a course. What if you wanted to find out which departments had never sent their staff members on a course? In some systems this problem is overcome by inserting a dummy record just to keep the missing data on file, but this in turn leads to other difficulties.

This kind of problem is known as a 'deletion anomaly'.

- If a member of staff has attended only one course and you inadvertently delete the row for that course, you will lose all information about that staff member.

The main reason why these problems occur is the fact that a single list is being used to keep information about more than one thing. In this simple example we can see that the file is storing information about:

- the staff members who are attending courses

- the departments in which those staff members work

- the courses that are being offered

- the actual attendance of an employee on a course (who is attending what course on what date).

The problems outlined above could be avoided if it was possible to keep the information about each of these things separately, and then make cross-references where required. This is the approach taken in a relational database.

The relational database approach

In a relational database, the data values held are stored in tables. Conceptually a table is an arrangement of rows and columns, just like a spreadsheet. However, one of the main advantages of a database over a spreadsheet is its ability to set up and automatically maintain cross-references between the tables. These cross-references are called 'relationships'.

The ability to create these relationships is not what gives the relational database its name.

The name relational comes from the fact that the inventor of the relational model, Dr E F Codd, decided to call the structure that holds the data a 'relation'. The common term for this structure is a table. Dr Codd also invented new words for the parts of the structure – a row is called a 'tuple' and a column is called an 'attribute'. These terms are seldom seen outside academic texts.

Despite the fact that a relational database uses a familiar arrangement of rows and columns to store data, it is not always obvious how best to divide the data up to create these tables. The process of designing a database involves determining what information the database needs to provide to its users, then deciding how best to partition the data into the tables and relationships that define the database structure.

Rules in a database are often referred to as constraints.

A database can be designed in such a way as to eliminate these initial problems. In addition, the database design can implement rules that can ensure the quality of the information that can be retrieved. These rules can be used to limit the values that can be entered into a column in a table. Identifying and documenting these rules is all part of the design process.

Poor database designs are often the result of a desire to start building the database before the requirements are known and a solution found. Users can become entranced by the technology to the extent that they lose sight of the fact that it is a means to an end, not an end in itself.

A systematic approach to database design

Implementing a large information system can be an extremely complicated process. Like all such endeavours, you are more likely to succeed if you can break down the work that needs to be done into a series of steps, and then break down each step into a series of manageable tasks.

This is the principle of divide and conquer at work. It is used in many disciplines associated with IT, including computer programming.

Rather than being overwhelmed by the size and complexity of the overall project, you can work through each of the tasks methodically. As the tasks are manageable, it is possible to monitor the progress of the work and quickly see if there are any problems.

The chances of successfully implementing a quality information system are increased by following a set of orderly steps, and using established techniques at each step. The basic steps to be followed during the design and construction of a database system are as follows.

1. Decide what is the purpose of the database.

2. Determine the information requirements of the database.

3. Produce a logical model of the information requirements of the database. A logical model is one that is not tied to a particular method of implementation. It describes the essential information requirements of the system, not the way that it will be constructed.

4. Convert the logical data model to a physical data model appropriate to the technology being used. (The logical design may have to be changed to suit the technology chosen.)

5. Implement the physical design using the chosen method or product.

The first of these steps is discussed in detail below. The other steps are explained below but discussed in more detail in the next six units.

1. Decide what is the purpose of the database

Like most things in life, designing a database is a process that involves choices and decisions. Decisions are much easier to make if you have objective criteria or goals against which you can measure the effectiveness of the choices available to you. When you decide what the purpose of the database is, you are setting the goal against which these choices can be evaluated.

Books on motivational theory tell us that the best goals are SMART goals. This acronym stands for:

Specific

Measurable

Achievable

Relevant

Time related.

- A specific goal for the course information system could be that it should be "a system that stores all the required data to enable the automated processing of course provider, attendee and enrolment information".

- A measurable goal would be "the cost of implementing the system should not exceed £5,000".

- An achievable goal for a database is one that is feasible given external and internal constraints. The goal "to eliminate the need for any manual processing of course enrolments' may not be achievable if the necessary computer hardware is not available at all times that course enrolments are to be recorded.

- Any goal must be relevant to the task at hand. A goal of "reducing the number of no-shows for course bookings" is not likely to be achieved solely by the implementation of a database system for recording course offerings and attendances.

- The best goals specify a time frame in which they should be achieved. If you need a new system to be operational within two weeks, it is going to affect the decisions that are to be made later about what is to be included in the system. Such time constraints are often imposed by people in an organisation other than the designers of the database, or even by agencies outside an organisation such as the government or other regulatory authorities.

Organisations often grade requirements using classifications such as essential, desirable and excluded.

At the end of this process it should be clear to all involved what is to be achieved and the constraints (both in terms of time and money) that impose limitations on what can be realistically achieved. It should also be clear what is not included within the scope of this particular development. Armed with this information all efforts can be directed at achieving the objectives for the system.

People other than the designers of the database often determine the overall requirements for a database. For example, the ultimate users of the system may decide what is required. Alternatively, business analysts in a separate part of the organisation, or even external consultants, may decide the purpose of the database.

Even if you don't decide the purpose yourself, you should evaluate the goals set by others to determine if they are SMART – especially if you will be making a commitment to achieving them.

2. Determine the information requirements of the database

Given the overall objectives for the database, it is now necessary to determine precisely what is required of the database. If you are lucky you may be given a detailed specification for the requirements of the database. More often, you will need to work out what is required. Determining the requirements for a database system is the subject of the next unit.

3. Produce a logical model of the information requirements of the database

A logical model is one that is independent of the technology that is used to implement it. However, given that you know that you are going to implement your system using Microsoft Access, isn't this unnecessary?

The answer to this question is, if you produce a model based on a belief that a system will be implemented in a particular way, you may introduce biases that make it difficult to make objective decisions. You may also run the risk of missing important requirements because it may not be possible to represent those requirements in the particular implementation method chosen. In addition, because you are not thinking about how you will actually construct the system, you can concentrate more on understanding what you are trying to achieve.

The techniques that are used to produce a logical data model are discussed in Units 4 and 5.

4. Convert the logical data model to a physical data model appropriate to the technology being used

Surely you can start building the database now? Sorry, not quite yet. It is usually the case that some changes need to be made to the design in order to make the most effective use of the particular product chosen for implementation. We also need to make a number of decisions about how the data itself will be represented in the system that we are going to implement.

The techniques that are used to produce a physical data model are discussed in Units 6 and 7.

5. Implement the physical design using the chosen product.

Finally you get to build the database! This is covered in Units 8 to 17.

Revision exercises

1. Less than 20 years ago only large companies could afford the types of system that could be used to run a database system. The PC has changed this. Now, home users of PCs often create database systems. Describe three applications in which you personally could benefit from a database system.

2. Write down some SMART goals that could be used to evaluate the requirements for one of these systems.

3. Describe the problems that can occur when redundant or inconsistent data is stored in a database.

4. What are the benefits of producing a logical design for a database before implementing the requirements using a particular product?

3 Determining requirements for a database system

What you will learn in this unit

This unit describes methods that you can use to help understand the requirements for a new database system. At the end of this unit you should:

❏ appreciate that before creating a new database system you must have a thorough understanding of the requirements for a new system

❏ understand the techniques that can be used for gathering information about requirements for a new database system

❏ understand the advantages and disadvantages of each of these techniques

❏ appreciate the type of information that is relevant to the task of creating a new database system.

Collecting data about requirements

A sure sign that a system has failed to meet its requirements is the continued use of old methods instead of, or in addition to, the new system.

Even if you are automating a process that you know very well (for example, you are creating a database for your own use or for your department's use), you should step back and think about what is required from a system based on a database. If you do not, you may end up simply automating the current way of doing things and miss opportunities for improvements or enhancements.

If you do not know the requirements for a new database system, there are a number of techniques that can be used to collect the necessary information. These involve:

• general information about an organisation

• specific information about the activities of the department or section of the organisation requiring a new system

• existing system documentation, files and output

• forms and other documents used in the organisation.

General information about an organisation

If you are new to an organisation you will benefit from an overview of the structure and activities of the organisation. Useful background information can be obtained from a number of published sources. Sources of information that are publicly available include:

- annual reports

- corporate brochures

- marketing literature.

Internal sources of information include:

- the organisation's mission statement

- the strategic plan, or other long-range planning documents

- policy manuals

- standard operating procedures

- organisation charts

- job descriptions.

Specific information about the activities of the department

Having obtained an overview of the organisation, you will need to obtain information about the activities of the department or section of the organisation that requires the system along with more specific information about the requirements for the system. There are a number of techniques that can be used for this:

- interviews

- group workshops

- questionnaires

- observations.

Interviews

An interview is a conversation with the aim of collecting detailed information from a person. Interviews are normally conducted one on one, and will often take place at the interviewee's work-place. This makes it easier for the interviewee to show examples to illustrate points being made.

The background information that you obtain by research can often make the task of conducting an interview easier.

Points to bear in mind about interviewing include the following:

- **Make adequate preparations before the interview.** Ensure that you have enough background information about the organisation or department concerned to conduct an intelligent conversation. Try to familiarise yourself with any technical terms that may come up in the interview.

- **Determine who should be interviewed.** You may be able to do this yourself based on your knowledge of the organisation, or as a result of reading the background information mentioned in the previous section. Often, however, the people to interview will be nominated by management within the organisation and protocol may dictate that you interview them in a particular order (such as in order of seniority).

- **Organise yourself in advance.** Make a note of the points that you want to cover and the key questions you want to ask in advance of the interview. If necessary rearrange the points to create a more logical ordering.

- **Schedule the interviews.** Contact the interviewee (or his or her assistant) to obtain an appointment for the interview. Explain the purpose of the interview, the areas to be covered, and how long it should take. When the arrangements have been agreed, confirm them in writing. In some cases you may want to send the interviewee a list of the points to be covered so that they can prepare themselves and obtain any relevant documents or reports.

- **Put the interviewee at ease.** Ensure that you arrive on time for the interview. First introduce yourself and then explain the purpose of the interview once again. Confirm how long the interview is to take. Bear in mind that some people may view the introduction of a computerised system as a threat to their position or status and may react negatively. If you intend to make notes, obtain the interviewee's approval. Tape recording an interview is not recommended as it may intimidate the interviewee.

- **Ask open-ended questions.** In an interview you will obtain the most information if the interviewee does most of the talking. An open-ended question is one that cannot be answered with a simple yes or no. Compare "Do course attendees pay a fine when they fail to attend?" with "What happens if someone fails to attend a course after enrolling?" Open-ended questions begin with words such as what, how, why, in what way, and so on. Of course, there will be some questions to which a yes or no answer would be the most appropriate.

- **Use appropriate language.** Make sure that you do not use words that may be perceived as judgemental or are emotionally charged. Phrases such as "inadequately controlled", "bureaucratic process" and so on may not be well received. Of course, it is quite valid for the interviewee to use such phrases. You should also avoid jargon or technical terms with which the interviewee may not be familiar. The aim of the interview is to obtain information, not to demonstrate your expertise in a technical area.

- **Ensure that you have understood the answer.** Make sure that you listen to what is being said. This may sound obvious, but the task of taking notes can be very distracting. You may also miss important visual clues such as body language while writing notes. Restate the interviewee's response to ensure that you have understood it correctly.

Rephrase statements and clarify ambiguous terms. If you do not understand a technical term, ask the interviewee to explain what it means.

- **Ask for examples.** If the interviewee makes a general observation, ask for an example of this in practice. Being specific will help you to understand the point and grasp differences and similarities between concepts.

- **Do not interrupt.** One of the easiest ways to stop someone from speaking openly is to interrupt him/her repeatedly.

- **Keep the interview on track.** One problem with open-ended questions is that they may encourage the interviewee to wander away from the topic. In addition, a request for an example may result in a long discussion of a particular event that occurred recently. If you have advised the interviewee of the points to be covered, you can suggest moving on to ensure that all items are dealt with. If such prompts to move on fail, it may be better to miss some of the final points than to appear rude.

- **Follow up the interview.** If appropriate, write to the interviewee to thank them for their time. If they have promised to send you further information or documents you can use this letter to jog their memory. If you find that some of the points made during the interview require clarification, you can request this at the same time.

Problems with interviews

Although interviews are a very effective way of obtaining information from people in an organisation, there are a number of problems that may lead you to consider alternative information gathering techniques.

- Conducting interviews can be extremely time-consuming and therefore costly.

- Collating the information can be time-consuming, and therefore costly.

- Separate interviews may lead to conflicting opinions and priorities.

- The people who are most knowledgeable about a particular area may be too busy to be interviewed.

- Interviews may be impractical due to the location of the interviewees.

- The information provided by interviewees may be misleading due to a fear of change, or other reasons such as office politics.

- The success of an interview depends greatly on the interpersonal skills of the individuals concerned.

Group workshops

A group workshop is a structured meeting in which representative groups of people who can define requirements for a new system come together for an extended period of time.

The aim is essentially the same as an interview, but since all the participants are together at the same time any conflicts of opinion can be clarified on the spot. The meeting may last for several hours, or even extend over more than one day, but the overall process should take less time than a series of separate interviews.

Group workshops may need to be organised and facilitated by more than one person. One person trained in workshop facilitation techniques may lead the discussion and serve as moderator while another may record the results of the discussion, document action points and so on.

Proponents of the group workshops say that, when used correctly, not only can they lead to more accurate requirements definition, but also to greater involvement of and commitment from the ultimate users of the system.

Group workshops have formed part of many methodologies, the most well known of which is probably Joint Application Design (JAD), developed by IBM.

Problems with group workshops

However, there are several problems with the group workshop technique.

- The technique requires extensive training for the facilitator.

- As a result of the time involved, the task of attending the sessions may be delegated to less knowledgeable personnel.

- The cost of bringing the participants together for a long period may be high.

Questionnaires

A questionnaire is a specially structured document used to collect facts and opinions from respondents. One advantage of questionnaires is that you can send them to many more people than it would be possible to interview or invite to a group workshop.

The are two main types of questionnaire: free format and fixed format. A free format questionnaire may resemble a list of open-ended interview questions that are written down with a space after each in which the respondent can record their answer. Free format questionnaires are seldom used because:

- it is often difficult to phrase such questions in an unambiguous way

- such questionnaires require a lot of time and effort on the part of the respondent

- it can be very time-consuming to collate the responses.

A fixed format questionnaire contains closed questions that require specific responses. Respondents are required to choose from a limited number of available responses. This can be a problem if the list of available responses does not include all the possible options, but it does make the task of collating results much easier.

The four main types of fixed format questions are as follows:

- **Simple yes/no questions.** A question such as "Do course attendees pay a fine when they fail to attend?" is an example of a question that could have a yes or no response. Notice, however, that the correct response may be "yes, but not for reasons of sickness".

- **Multiple choice.** A question such as "What is the average number of attendees per course?" could offer options between one and six.

- **Rating.** Rating questions are a way of quantifying opinions, offering options such as 'strongly agree', 'agree', 'no opinion', 'disagree', and 'strongly disagree'.

- **Ranking.** A question such as "Rank the following activities according to the amount of your time spent processing them" could offer a selection of activities with a space against each for the respondent to indicate a percentage of their time.

Before you send out a questionnaire, test it out on a small sample of respondents. This may bring to light a number of ambiguities or omissions. When you send questionnaires to respondents you should include information such as:

- why they are being asked the questions

- who is asking them

- what the replies will be used for

- who else is being asked.

Problems with questionnaires

The use of questionnaires can eliminate many of the time delays and costs associated with interviewing. However, there are several disadvantages associated with using questionnaires.

- Good questionnaires are difficult to prepare.

- The number of people who respond to a questionnaire is often low.

- Questionnaires tend to be inflexible. You must be sure you are asking the right questions in advance. In an interview situation you can drop an entire line of questioning if it proves to be irrelevant.

- The answers given may be incomplete, unclear or invalid. There is no opportunity to clarify such answers.

- Collating the results can be very time-consuming.

- Separate questionnaires may lead to conflicting opinions and priorities.

Observation

Observation of a process can be used to clarify requirements and to gain an understanding of the workplace environment. The options for a new system may be constrained by the physical environment in which the work takes

Observations of people doing their job can be useful, but you should bear in mind that people's behaviour may change if they know that they are being watched.

place. For example, a solution involving barcoding may not be feasible if there is no physical space for a barcode reader at the point where, for example, course enrolments take place.

Existing system documentation, files and output

If an automated, or partially automated, system already exists it can provide a fertile source of information about the data used by an organisation.

However, you must be careful to ensure that you do not simply reproduce the current system using a different platform or product.

Problems with using existing system documentation

Small systems developed by individuals using products such as a spreadsheet are seldom documented at all.

There are various problems involved in using exiting system documentation

- Documentation may be out of date and may not accurately reflect the current state of the system.

- Data files may include data or storage space for data that is no longer used.

- The output may no longer be used. Reports may be produced and simply filed away.

- The same data may appear in different places on the system with different names, prefixes or acronyms.

- It can be easy to get bogged down in an analysis of the current system.

Forms and other documents used in the organisation

If the process to be automated is currently implemented as a manual system, the existing paper-based forms can also be a fertile source of information about the data used by an organisation.

When looking at forms, bear the following points in mind.

- Items on the form that change each time the form is completed may represent data items that need to be stored in the database system.

- There is not necessarily a one-to-one mapping between items on a form and the data items to be stored. For example, a form to gather survey data may include multiple choices indicated by tick boxes. Only one of the boxes would be ticked at any one time. A database design should not include a data item for each possible value represented by the tick boxes. Instead it would include a single data item that would hold the value represented by the selected item.

- Items on the form that are derived by calculation may not become data items to be stored in the database.

- Not every item on the form may still be needed. An organisation may still use a preprinted form, even though some of the requirements for its use may have changed.

- Items that have different names on different forms may actually be the same thing.

Results of requirements analysis

At the end of the requirements analysis you will have accumulated lots of information about the organisation and its needs for a database system. In its raw form it may not be all that useful. The next step is to organise and collate the information that you have accumulated.

The database in CASE products may be referred to as a data dictionary or a repository.

If you are thinking that this task of organising data about the data sounds like a job for a database, you are right – it is. Most Computer Aided Software Engineering (CASE) tools provide such a database to store just this type of information. From the data you have accumulated you will need to extract the following information:

- Information about the data that needs to be stored

- Information about business rules

- Information about operational requirements.

Information about the data that needs to be stored

You will have identified many data items that the database may or may not be required to store. Later in this unit we will look at the need to provide a logical and unique name for each item to be stored. In addition to a name for each data item, you may also want to record the following.

- **Where does the data come from?** You may find that a data item originates in another computer system, such as a mainframe, and is manipulated in a spreadsheet prior to being used in the environment currently being studied.

- **Where is it used?** You may find that the data item is not used at all.

- **What range of values can it hold?** What are the minimum and maximum values that it can hold (this is often referred to as a domain). Is there a value that is assigned to the data item automatically if no other value is specified?

- **How it is changed?** Does the data item's value remain constant after entry into the system or does some form of processing change it?

- **When can it be deleted?** Some data items exist only temporarily while others may need to remain for a set period of time before being deleted or archived.

- **Who is allowed to create, see, change or delete it?** There may be a security requirement to prevent deliberate or inadvertent misuse of the data item.

- **How does it relate to other data?** Some data items may require the presence of other data items to be useful or correct.

The more you understand the nature of the data and how it is used, the easier the subsequent steps in the process become.

Information about business rules

Such rules are generally called business rules, even if they occur in an organisation that, strictly speaking, is not a business at all.

All organisations whether they are commercial, institutional or governmental have a number of rules that govern the way they work. It may be possible to implement some of these rules in the database. Others may have to be implemented in application programs that use the database, or even as policies or working procedures.

Some rules may seem obvious, but may easily be overlooked when the time comes to implement the database. For example, a company would not normally employ somebody unless it had sufficient information about the person being employed. This would include their National Insurance number, the person's date of birth, the receipt of a reference, and so on. Another rule may be that employees may only attend a training course if they have met the prerequisites for the course.

Information about operational requirements

It is important to know the operational requirements for any new database system. Operational requirements should include the following points.

- **The number of users who may need to use the system**. You should know how many users will need to be able to use the database at the same time (concurrent access) as well as the overall number of users. In addition, will this increase over time?

- **The location of users of the database.** Will users be connected to the database via a Local Area Network (LAN), or via a Wide Area Network (WAN) or a dial-up connection?

- **What volume of throughput is required?** The answer to this may be expressed as the number of transactions that the system will have to cope with. You should have an average number of transactions per hour or per day, as well as a maximum figure for peak periods. Once again, will this increase over time?

- **What response time is expected for commonly used transactions?**

- **What type of availability is required of a new system?** Availability is usually expressed using two measures. Mean Time Between Failures (MTBF) is a measure of how frequently a system is unavailable. Mean

Time To Recover (MTTR) is a measure of how long it takes to fix a broken system.

- **What security controls are required for the system as a whole?**

In some ways understanding operational requirements can be the key to the implementation of a successful system. A system can meet all of the data storage requirements of an organisation but still be abandoned if the response time is too slow or it breaks down frequently.

In Units 8 to 17 we use Microsoft Access to show how a database design can be implemented. Access is an excellent product to create databases for use on a single PC, or for use by up to 20 or so concurrent users on a LAN. If a system requires concurrent access by more than this number of users, or access over a WAN, it is most likely that you will need a different product.

Naming data items

When recording the requirements for an information system it is necessary to identify everything about which the system is required to store or process information. This is normally accomplished by assigning a name to each item. Deciding what to call things can be more of a problem than you might at first expect.

The problem with names

Data items identified during data analysis need to be distinguished by the use of a unique and logical name. As you look more closely you may find that the names currently used in the organisation (or in an existing system) do not meet these requirements. In the real world we use names to identify people, places and things. In an ideal world all names would be unique so there would be no possibility of confusion. However, this is not always possible.

When the same name is used to identify different things we can rely on context to resolve the ambiguity. Since I live in Croydon, Surrey, when I say the word Croydon I am more likely to be referring to that place than to the Croydon in New South Wales, Australia. Unfortunately, computers cannot imply a context for a name that is ambiguous.

Problems with using existing names

Although it is preferable to use the names that are familiar to the intended users of a system, it is not always possible. A number of problems can arise from using existing names.

The same name is used for different things

Common sense dictates that the names given to different things should also be different. Imagine the confusion if we only had one word to describe, for example, a container for liquids. Rather than being able to use a word that describes the item precisely (such as cup, mug, beaker, glass, tumbler and so on), we would have to give a full description in order to be precise. We would have to resort to phrases such as "the small earthenware container with the handle", or risk getting our tea in a wine glass!

When recording requirements for a system, however, it is very easy to use the same name for things that are logically different. This can occur in the following scenarios.

- **When only part of a name is used.** For example, often we will need to hold a description of something about which we need to store data. We could end up with a number of different data items all called Description. In order to avoid confusion, it is better to use a more complete name that includes the name of the thing that the description refers to, such as Subject Description or Format Description.

The technical term used to describe the circumstance when the same name is used for different things is homonym.

- **When technical jargon is adopted as a name.** Quite often different parts of an organisation use the same term to refer to quite different things. For example, in an export company the term ShippedDate might be used by one department to mean the date that an item left the company's warehouse. At the same time another department might use the same term to refer to the date that the ship on which the item was transported left the harbour. In this example more precise names such as DateExWarehouse and DateExHarbour could be adopted to resolve the problem.

- **When excessive abbreviation is used.** In the past limitations of the hardware or operating system could lead to excessive abbreviation of names (in most DOS-based databases names for tables were limited to eight characters).

A different name is used for the same thing

This can occur if different parts of the same organisation use different names to refer to the same thing. The same data may be called two different things on different forms used within an organisation. This can also occur if the designers of an existing system have not made an effort to be consistent with the names used. This can lead to communication problems between the different parts of the organisation and between the designers of a database and its ultimate users. It can also lead to redundancy in the design of a database (the same data being held more than once in the same table, or in different tables).

The technical term used to describe the circumstance when the same name is used for different things is synonym.

Resolving this problem can cause political problems in an organisation, especially if you try to get one department to change the word that it uses to the term used by another department. Fortunately, most database software provides ways to use consistent names for fields internally, while presenting different labels for them to the users. This can overcome the problem without upsetting the users of the system.

The name used does not accurately describe the data held

When asked to convert an existing database you can often come across the problem where the name of a field in a table bears absolutely no relationship to the meaning of the data held in it.

This can occur if the design of the existing database should have been changed to reflect a change in requirements. However, a 'quick fix' may have been implemented by reusing an existing field to hold a completely different data item. It can also occur if the person designing the database did not fully understand the meaning of the data being stored and incorrectly used a technical term as the name of a field.

If you are given the task of converting or upgrading an existing computerised system, it pays to be sceptical about the current design. Do not assume that the names used in an existing system accurately describe the data that is actually stored!

Guidelines for naming data elements

You can avoid most of these problems if you adopt the following guidelines when naming data items.

- Do not use abbreviations unless absolutely necessary.

- Expand on generic names. For example, a field on a form may just say Date. You can resolve ambiguity by qualifying the name as Course Start Date, or Course End Date.

- Add a question mark to the name of a data item that holds a yes or no value.

- If you are forced to choose one name from many possible names in an organisation, keep a record of the alternative names for cross-referencing purposes.

Ensuring good naming standards

In many organisations a particular person is given responsibility for ensuring that the names used in database designs are appropriate. This person is usually called the data administrator. In a large organisation this may be a full-time job; in smaller organisations it may be one of many roles performed by one individual (usually in the Information Technology department).

The role of the data administrator can be a political one. As mentioned before, trying to get one part of an organisation to change the terms that they use can be seen as unneeded interference. Worse, in some organisations, the role of data administrator may be seen as an attempt by the IT Department to wrest back control of IT that was lost with the introduction of desktop computers.

If the role of data administration exists in your organisation, you should attempt to ensure that the names that you use in your database comply with the standards set down.

Organisations using data administrators have had most success in ensuring consistency in large systems affecting the whole organisation. Smaller, departmental systems (many of them implemented in Microsoft Access) tend to be more affected by the problems outlined above.

Please remember, the role of a data administrator is quite different to the role of database administrator. Data administration is a non-technical role for defining standards that are independent of a particular technology. In contrast, a database administrator is given responsibility for the physical implementation and maintenance of a database using a particular Database Management System.

Naming standards for Microsoft Access

As mentioned in Unit 1, an Access database contains a number of different objects – tables, queries, forms, reports and so on. Using Access it is quite possible to give the same name to different objects. For example, you could have a table named Customer, a query called Customer, and a form called Customer. As a database gets larger this can cause considerable problems.

To avoid these problems a number of individuals who earn their living from building commercial Access applications have developed and published naming standards for Access objects. The best known of these was developed by Stan Leszynski and it can be found in a number of books about Access.

Although the use of these naming standards can ease the task of developing a database in Microsoft Access, they should not be used for defining the logical requirements for a system, which should be independent of any particular implementation method.

Revision exercises

The training department in Castellan has a requirement for another database. The department holds an assortment of training materials (books, videos and multimedia titles) that can be used on their courses or loaned to other departments. A system is required to maintain data on the titles that are held and to keep track of loans of the material to other departments.

1. What techniques do you think would be most appropriate to determine the requirements for such a system?

2. Make a list of internal documents or publications that may assist you in finding out background information for such a system.

3. You have decided that you need to interview the training manager to determine her requirements. Make a list of the questions that would be appropriate for such an interview.

4. Design a questionnaire that could be used to obtain the same information from a larger audience.

4 Creating the data model

What you will learn in this unit

This unit describes how to create a logical data model for a new system using Entity-Relationship diagrams. At the end of this unit you should:

❏ understand the components that make up an Entity-Relationship (E-R) diagram

❏ understand how to identify these components from the requirements defined for the system

❏ understand how more complicated requirements are modelled in an Entity-Relationship diagram

❏ be able to draw simple Entity-Relationship diagrams

❏ understand how Computer Aided Software Engineering (CASE) tools can be used to help in the process of creating a data model.

Why produce a data model?

After gathering requirements for a database system you may find that you have an almost daunting amount of information. Before you can begin to implement the requirements in a database, it is necessary to make some sense of this complexity. One way to do this is to construct a data model.

A model is an abstract representation of something that exists in the real world. Models are used extensively in other disciplines to make something that is complex understandable and to communicate information in an easily understandable format. For example, architects use three dimensional scale models to give an overall impression of a building or development and electrical engineers use schematic diagrams to depict the design of electrical circuits. ER diagrams are one of a number of methods for representing the data requirements for an information system.

In Unit 2 we saw how problems can arise from poor structure in a database. In fact, the majority of these problems arose because one Excel list was being used to hold information about a number of different things. The main purpose of E-R modelling is to identify and document each separate item about which data needs to be held in the system, and to identify and document how these items are related to each other for cross-referencing purposes. The technique also allows you to identify what individual items of data need to be held in each of the entities that have been identified.

Entity-Relationship modelling

E-R diagrams have become the most widely used technique for modelling the data requirements for an information system. On the basis that "a picture is worth a thousand words", an E-R model uses graphical representations of the things that are important in a system. In fact we could use pictures to depict the things that we need to include in the model, as in Figure 4.1.

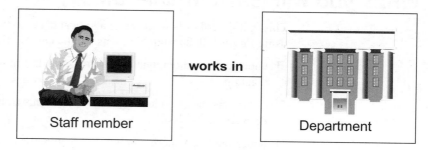

Fig 4.1
A pictorial representation of two entities in a system

However, pictorial representations like this can cause problems because we can be distracted by the artistic qualities (or otherwise) of the pictures. In addition, it can be difficult to find pictures that are instantly recognisable as the concepts that we are trying to represent. Figure 4.1 uses the picture of a building to represent a department, but it could be interpreted as representing an office or some other type of building such as a bank. It would be even more difficult to find pictures to represent an abstract concept such as a supplier or customer. To avoid this problem an E-R diagram uses symbols to represent the components of the model.

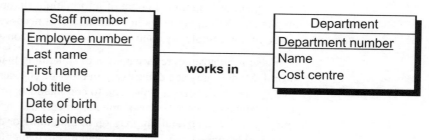

Fig 4.2
A symbolic representation of two entities in a system

The main components of an E-R model are:

- **Entities.** An entity is any thing of significance about which information needs to be held. Entities may be real objects, such as a book; they may be people, such as a staff member, or they may be events or abstract concepts, such as an enrolment on a course offering. The name of the entity is indicated in the top part of the box.

- **Attributes** An attribute is any item of data that can be used to identify, classify, quantify, qualify or describe the state of an entity. For example, an entity that represents a person may have attributes such as Name, Age, Sex and so on. Each of the items in the bottom part of the boxes is an attribute of that entity.

- **Relationships** A relationship is a significant real world association between entities. For example, there is a real world association between a staff member and a department – the staff member works in the department. The line between the two boxes in the diagram represents a relationship.

The key objectives of E-R modelling are:

- to provide an accurate model of the data that an organisation needs to obtain and store

- to enable these requirements to be communicated in a non-technical language

- to produce a model that is independent of any method of implementation. In other words, to produce a model that can be implemented using different techniques that may or may not involve a database, and perhaps may not even require a computer.

It is important to realise that an E-R diagram does not represent the flow of data through a system. It simply represents how the items about which data has to be stored fit together. As a result the diagram can be read in any direction – from right to left, or left to right; from bottom to top or from top to bottom.

There are many different notations for drawing E-R diagrams. Different methodologies (and tools) use different symbols to represent the components of a diagram. Although the symbols differ, the concepts are the same. This book uses the Information Engineering Method-ology conventions

Defining entities

Your model should include an entity for everything of significance about which data needs to be held. However, this is easier said than done. You need to analyse the data about the requirements for the system to determine which things are significant and which are not. Problems may result from the fact that people often talk in terms of examples – they may talk in terms of roles such as job titles, or use individual place names, or use the technical jargon of their particular profession.

For example, in an interview for the Castellan system the training manager may describe how accounts clerks are interested in the bookkeeping course run by Learning Labs, while IT support engineers are interested in the Windows courses run by CompuLearn. The words used do not describe the entities that need to be modelled. Instead they are words that represent specific examples of entities. In this example each job title (accounts clerk, training manager) is an example of a more general entity that we can call

An entity must represent a type or class of thing, not a particular example of that thing.

Staff member. Course titles (book-keeping, Windows) are examples of a general entity that we can call Course, and the names of the different training companies indicate an entity called a Course provider. Part of the process of creating the model involves generalising entities from the specific examples provided.

You may also find that some of the information gathered during requirements definition is not relevant to the data model. Provided that the purpose of the system has been clearly defined it should be easy to decide what is relevant and what is not. For example, during the Castellan interview the training manager may have described how course delegates prefer the meal options provided by Learning Labs to other external course providers. This is only relevant if one of the requirements for the system is to record employee ratings for the providers of external courses.

When defining a data model there is no substitute for experience, common sense and continuous communication with the people who know the information requirements of the organisation. What can make the task particularly difficult is the need to determine the essential from the particular, and to recognise what is relevant amongst a wealth of detail.

The first step in creating the model is to produce a simple list of all the entities that will need to appear in the diagram. Part of the process of producing this list is deciding what to call each entity.

Naming entities

E-R diagrams should be treated as a means to an end, not as an end product in themselves. Ensuring that the diagram accurately repre-sents the data requirements of the system is more important than the artistic qualities of the diagram.

The name of an entity should reflect the fact that it represents a type or class or item, not a particular instance of that item. You should use a noun, or group of nouns, that describes the person, object, event or location that the entity represents. Examples of entity names include Course, Staff member, Course provider, Department and so on.

Once you have produced the initial list of entities you can set about creating the first draft of the diagram. You should not expect to get the diagram right first time. If you have to produce the diagram on paper make sure that you use a pencil and have an eraser to hand.

Representing entities

An entity is represented on the diagram as a rectangular box. The name of the entity appears in the top section of the rectangle.

Fig 4.3
An entity is represented on the diagram by a box

Defining attributes

An attribute is any data item that can be used to identify, classify, quantify, qualify or describe the state of an entity. During the requirements gathering you will have identified many data items that may need to be held in the system. The task here is to match each data item to the particular entity that it describes. As part of this task you should ensure the following.

- **Each attribute represents a single data item.** You may have identified data items that are actually compound data values. For example, you may wish to store a person's name. In fact this data item may consist of a first name, a last name and possibly an initial. You should represent these as separate attributes of an entity. When it comes to implementing the data model it may be important to be able to manipulate the individual components of the compound data item. For example, you may need to search on, or sort by, the person's last name. This would be extremely difficult if this component was held as part of a compound data item. Addresses are another example of compound data items that should be broken down into their separate constituents or attributes.

The next unit describes techniques that can be used to verify that an attribute is in the correct entity.

- **Each attribute describes the entity to which it has been allocated.** Ensuring that each attribute is in the right place will prevent redundant duplication of data items. In some cases this will be easy (it is fairly obvious that the data item for an employee's last name should be included as an attribute of the Staff member entity). In other cases you may be faced with a more difficult choice. You may find that as the model develops you will have to move attributes from one entity to another.

- **Each attribute should not represent data that can be derived from other attributes.** The decision whether to calculate derived data at the time that the data is displayed or to hold derived data permanently in the system should be made at the time that the system is actually implemented. Any data items that can be derived from calculations performed on other data items should not appear on the data model.

Naming attributes

The name of an attribute should be a simple, singular noun. In an E-R model the attribute name should not include the name of the entity. Examples of attribute names include Title, First name, Postcode and Part number.

Representing attributes

Attributes are listed in the lower part of the rectangle that represents the entity to which they belong.

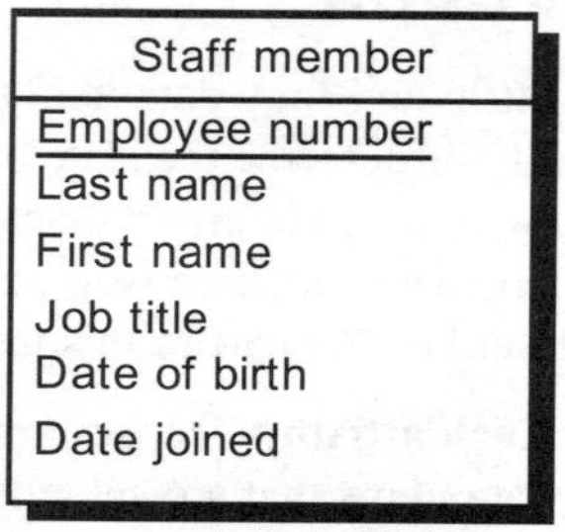

```
                    ┌─────────────────────────┐
                    │      Staff member       │
                    ├─────────────────────────┤
                    │ Employee number         │
                    ├─────────────────────────┤
                    │ Last name               │
                    │ First name              │
                    │ Job title               │
                    │ Date of birth           │
                    │ Date joined             │
                    └─────────────────────────┘
```

Fig 4.4
Attributes of an
entity are listed in
the bottom part of
the box

Choosing a unique identifier for each entity

In the E-R diagram the
attribute (or
attributes) that serves
as the unique identifier
for the entity is
underlined.

Each entity in an E-R model must contain an attribute, or combination of attributes, that can be used to uniquely identify each instance of the entity. In other words, there must be an attribute, or combination of attributes, that distinguishes each occurrence of the entity from every other occurrence. For example, in the Staff member entity we need to hold a value that identifies a single member of staff from every other member of staff. A value for this attribute must be known for all instances of the entity and it must be guaranteed to be unique.

It is possible that an existing data item could be used to uniquely identify the entity. For example, an Employee number is designed to uniquely identify a member of staff. But couldn't we simply use the employee's full name as the unique identifier? In most cases this would not cause a problem. However, it is quite possible that two different members of staff could have the same name. Since it is necessary to be able to uniquely identify every staff member, an attribute that would work for most, but not all, is not good enough. If the full name is not enough, what about the combination of the staff member's name and their date of birth? The odds against two individuals with the same name and date of birth, both joining the same company, are pretty astronomical! However, this idea brings its own problems.

- In order to use this method you would have to know the date of birth of each and every staff member about whom you want to keep a record. If this information were not known it would not be possible to store information about that person. (More likely, an individual using such a system would simply make up a date of birth for this attribute in order to get around the problem.)

- Referring to the entity itself becomes long-winded. Imagine if you had to refer to a staff member as "the Dipak Patel who was born on 12 March 1957" every time you mentioned him. Just as it would take up a lot of your time in a conversation, this long-windedness can make the model unwieldy.

In the United Kingdom each resident may be identified by their National Health number, although a separate National Insurance number is used to identify the individuals who have reached working age.

To avoid this problem a unique but arbitrary value is created to identify the person or thing. This is exactly what an employee number is, a number invented for the sole purpose of identify each individual staff member. These invented identifiers are quite common in the real world. Governments have a need to identify each and every citizen in the country. To facilitate this they give each person a unique number. People are not the only things that have to be identified. Objects need to be identified, so companies use product numbers, part numbers and other similar codes to identify products.

In some cases there is no existing attribute in the data that we can use to uniquely identify the entity. In other cases we may not be certain that we will know the value of an attribute that could be used as a unique identifier in all possible cases. (Imagine having to ask all your customers for their National Health number, simply because the designer of the system had chosen this value as the unique identifier for an entity!) In these cases we may need to invent an arbitrary attribute that will hold a unique, but meaningless value, and will serve to identify the entity within the context of the system. This invented attribute would normally hold an arbitrary number chosen from a sequence, or generated at random. The value chosen is in itself not important as long as it is guaranteed to be unique.

Invented unique identifiers within a system are often referred to as synthetic or surrogate identifiers.

Defining relationships

Once you have drawn the entities and their attributes on the E-R diagram, it is time to decide how they fit together. A relationship on an E-R diagram represents a significant real world association between entities. Sometimes these are easy to recognise. For example, there is an obvious relationship between a staff member and a department – the staff member works in a department. Other relationships may not be so obvious.

There are common types of relationships that are often present in data models. One common relationship type is known as a 'whole-part' relationship. This is where one entity is made up of, or contains, multiple instances of another entity. For example, an organisation may be made up of a number of divisions and each division may consist of a number of departments. In a manufacturing environment an assembly may be made up of a number of different parts. Often these associations can be thought of as parent-child relationships.

Another common type of relationship is classification. One entity may serve to classify or categorise another entity. For example, we may want to categorise training courses into different types (such as courses related to health and safety or training in computer software packages). You may find it helpful to think of these as 'type-of' relationships, where one entity holds values that are the various types of the other entity.

Naming relationships

Relationships often, though not always, are named using verbs. For example, the relationship between a staff member and a department is that the staff member 'works' in a department. In fact, since a relationship has two ends it will have two names – one will usually be the active mode of the verb, the other the passive mode. The relationship between a department and a staff member is that the staff member is 'assigned to' a department.

A whole-part relationship may be described using the terms 'part of' and 'composed of'. For example, an order may be composed of many line items and each line item forms part of an order. A 'type-of' relationship may be described using the terms 'classifies' and 'classified by'. For example, a course type can be used to classify a course and a course is classified by a course type.

Representing relationships

A relationship is represented as a line between the boxes that represent the entities that it links.

Fig 4.5
Relationships are represented as a line between the two entities concerned

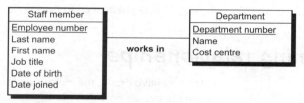

Further refining relationships

Including further information about each relationship can enhance the value of the model. For each end of a relationship we would like to know:

- Does the existence of the entity at one end of the relationship depend upon the existence of a corresponding example of the other entity? The technical term for this is the 'participation' in a relationship.

- How many instances of the entity can take part in the relationship at any one time? The technical term for this is the 'cardinality' of the relationship.

Participation

This need for an instance of one entity to exist before an instance of another entity can be created is often known as an 'existence dependency'.

In some cases business rules require that an instance of a particular entity must exist before instances of another, related entity can be created. For example, most organisations will insist that a customer's details have been entered into a system before the system will accept orders from that customer (accepting orders from unknown companies is likely to lead to bad debt problems). In our example we would want to ensure that a record of a department exists before we assign a member of staff to work in that department.

Cardinality

The number of instances of an entity that can take part in a relationship may be determined by the business rules for an organisation or by facts that exist in the real world. It is a fact that an employee will usually attend more than one course during their period of employment with a company. However, a company could have a business rule that said that an employee could only attend one course during the term of their employment (although this is extremely unlikely).

Representing cardinality and participation

A 'crows-foot' symbol at the end of a relationship line indicates the 'many' end of a relationship, while a single line represents the 'one' end of a relationship. A single vertical line across the end of a relationship line indicates mandatory participation in the relationship while the small circle at the end of the relationship line indicates optional participation in the relationship.

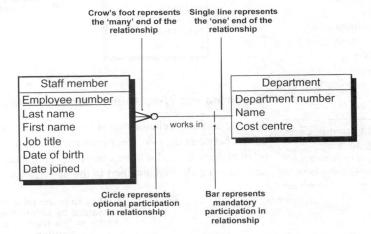

Fig 4.6
Cardinality and participation can be shown on the relationship line

The fragment from an E-R diagram shown in Figure 4.6 can be read as "many staff members work in one (and only one) department and each department employs one or more staff members".

Examples of invalid constructs in an E-R diagram

Some types of constructs are invalid in an E-R model. This may be because it is impossible for such a structure to exist in the real world, or it may be impossible to implement such a structure in an information system. These are the most common examples of invalid constructs.

Many-to-many relationships

Many-to-many relationships exist in the real world, but cannot be implemented in an information system. An example of a many-to-many relationship is that between a course offering and a staff member. Each staff member may attend many course offerings, and each course offering may be attended by many staff.

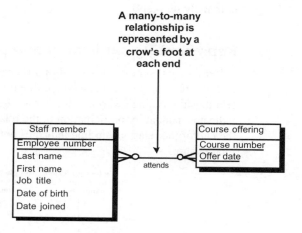

Fig 4.7
An example of an invalid many-to-many relationship

Resolving many-to-many relationships

An entity that resolves a many-to-many relationship is called an 'intersection entity'.

A many-to-many relationship is resolved by creating a third entity that comes between the two other entities. The cardinality of the two new relationships formed will be one on the side attached to the original entity and many on the end attached to the new entity.

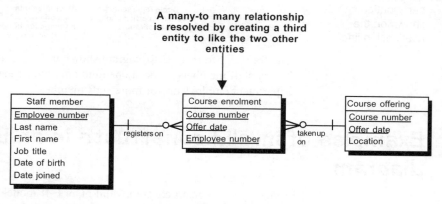

Fig 4.8
An intersection entity used to resolve the many-to-many relationship

Sometimes the new entity represents something that exists in the area being modelled. In Figure 4.8, the missing entity was the course enrolment, which records the particular staff member enrolling on the particular course offering. In this example the entity can be named after the thing that it represents. In other examples the name may be quite arbitrary. For example, in a personnel system we may want to keep a record of all the languages that a staff member can speak. Each staff member may be able to speak many languages and each language may be spoken by many staff members. The intersection entity that can be created to resolve this many-to-many relationship has no equivalent in the real world. The easiest way to name such entities is to use the combination of names of the other two entities involved – for example, Employee-Language.

Mandatory participation at both ends of a relationship

In an information system it is not possible to implement a relationship that is mandatory at both ends. For example, there may be a rule that says that every staff member must be assigned to a department and each department must have at least one staff member in it.

To implement such a rule a system you would need to be able to create a record for a department and a record for at least one staff member at exactly the same time. Since this is not possible, we will have broken the rule immediately each time we create a new department.

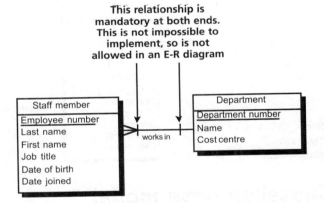

Fig 4.9
Mandatory participation at both ends of a relationship

Only represent direct relationships in the diagram

You should make sure that the E-R model only shows the direct relationships between two entities. For example, since one of the requirements of the Castellan system is to keep track of the departments that send individuals on courses, you may be tempted to draw a relationship between a department entity and a course attendance entity.

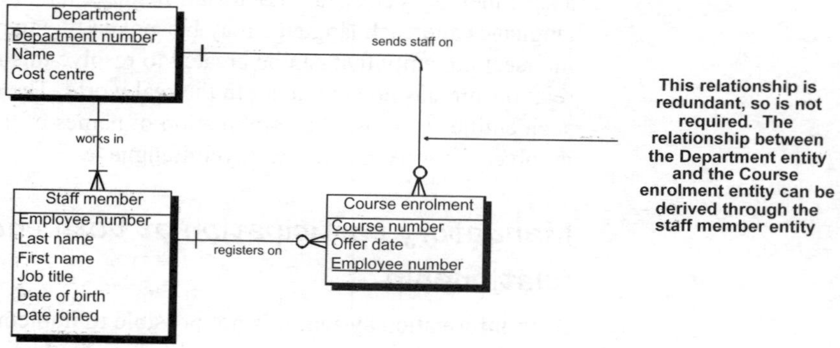

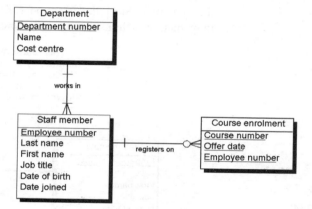

Fig 4.10
Indirect relationships that can be derived from other relationships should not be shown on the diagram

This relationship is redundant, so is not required. The relationship between the Department entity and the Course enrolment entity can be derived through the staff member entity

However, so long as we know which staff member attends a course as well as what department the staff member works for, we can derive this information.

Fig 4.11
The corrected diagram only shows the direct relationships

The Castellan data model

The E-R diagram Fig 4.12 shows the main components of the Castellan data model.

E-R diagrams for other systems may show many more entities than this. In some cases it is necessary to break down the model into sub-models to avoid being overwhelmed by the number of objects on the diagram.

The model in Figure 4.12 shows an example of a whole-part relationship (between the Department and Staff member entities) and a classification relationship (between the Course type and Course entities).

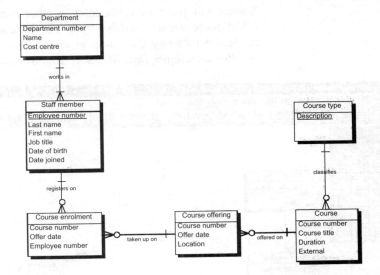

Fig 4.12
The main components
of the Castellan data
model

Using CASE tools for E-R modelling

Drawing E-R diagrams by hand can be extremely tedious. If the
requirements change during the analysis process it can be difficult to keep
the diagrams up to date and the process can become prone to errors. One
way to ease the pain of re-drawing E-R diagram is not to draw the diagram
on paper at all, but to use a standard index card to represent each entity.
Each attribute of the entity is then written on the lines on the card. The cards
can then be pinned on a board and the relationships represented by pieces of
string stretched between the pins. This primitive but effective technique
(known in some circles as Cardboard Aided Software Engineering) makes it
easy to move the entities around on the diagram.

Computer Aided Software Engineering (CASE) products are software
programs that can assist in the process of creating models of information
systems. CASE tools may contain a number of different components
including the following.

- A drawing tool for producing the E-R diagram.

- A data dictionary for recording information about each entity and the
  attributes they contain. In the best CASE tools the data dictionary is
  seamlessly integrated with the drawing tool.

- Tools for checking the completeness and correctness of the model.

- Some products also include tools for automatically generating a database
  (or even an application program) from the definitions held in the data
  dictionary.

Some CASE tools use methodologies other than E-R diagrams. Examples of CASE tools that are available for Windows-based PCs and that support E-R models include EasyCase from Visible Systems, ER-Win from Logic Works, and PowerDesigner Data Architect from Sybase.

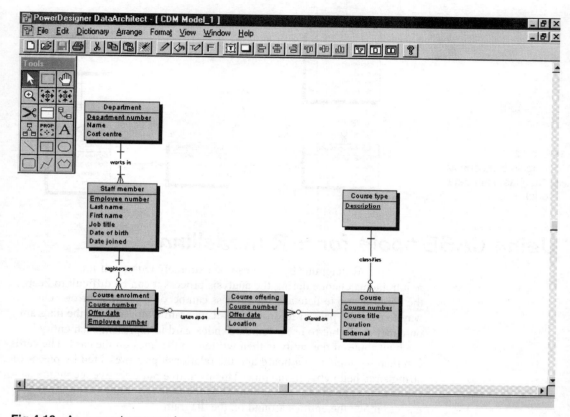

Fig 4.13 An example screen from the PowerDesigner Data Architect CASE product

Revision exercises

You have been provided with the requirements for the Castellan training materials system which are as follows. The system needs to keep a record of all the training materials that are held in the department for internal use, or for loan to other departments. The system will need to record whether the item held is a book, video, multimedia title or some other format, as well as the organisation from which the item was obtained. In some cases the training department will have more than one copy of the same title. The training manager wants to know what materials other departments have borrowed. If the item has not been returned she would like to know when it is due for return. Training materials can only be loaned to existing departments.

1. Draw an E-R diagram to represent these requirements. Your diagram should show the attributes as well as the unique identifier for each entity.

2. Books published in the United Kingdom are allocated a number to identify them (the International Standard Book Number – ISBN). If the training department only held books, would the ISBN number be a good attribute to uniquely identify a Book entity? Explain your answer.

3. What would be the main advantages of using a CASE tool to produce a data model? Can you think of any disadvantages?

5 Using normalisation to ensure design quality

What you will learn in this unit

This unit describes methods that you can use to ensure the quality of the data model to avoid the problems that can occur with a poor design. At the end of this unit you should:

❑ understand what normalisation is and how it relates to Entity-Relationship (E-R) modelling

❑ be able to describe first, second and third normal forms

❑ understand the methods that are used to convert entities that have not been normalised into their highest normal form

❑ understand the importance of choosing the appropriate unique identifier for an entity.

By understanding the requirements for a system you are able to produce a model of the data that it needs to hold using E-R diagrams. However, entities produced in this way may not be organised in the best possible way to implement the data model using a computerised system. You can use a process known as normalisation to ensure that your data model is organised in the optimal way.

What is normalisation?

Normalisation is a formal process based on mathematics which defines a set of rules for creating structures that are arranged in the best way to enable the storage and retrieval of data. Dr E F Codd defined the process in the early 1970s at the same time as he defined the relational model.

The normal forms are based on the requirement to model data in two-dimensional structures consisting of a variable number of rows and a variable number of columns. Codd called these structures relations, but

The name normalisation was borrowed from the political jargon of the time. The United States was attempting to resume normal relations with the People's Republic of China – a process known as normalisation. Codd adopted this name for the process.

almost all database products refer to them as tables. Relations have the following attributes:

- they describe one (and only one) entity

- each row is uniquely identifiable

- the order of the columns is not important

- the order of the rows is not important.

Modelling an organisation's data requirements as nothing more than a set of these two dimensional structures can be a challenge. Normalisation is a process that can be followed to determine the best arrangement of these structures in order to avoid possible problems when accessing or updating the data.

How does normalisation fit in with E-R modelling?

This unit discusses normalising entities, but the technique is often applied to existing tables in a database which are being converted to a relational product.

The techniques of E-R modelling and normalisation are not mutually exclusive. In fact the two techniques can be used together to produce a more complete and correct data model. Before normalisation can commence it is necessary to have a fairly complete list of all the data items that need to be held in the database. In theory it should be possible to start with a complete list of all the attributes in the system and start normalising. In large systems the sheer volume of data involved would make this impossible. In order to make the task of normalisation manageable, the attributes need to be organised into some preliminary groupings – in other words, entities. At the end of the process of normalisation you may need to revise your E-R model to show the normalised entities.

The process of breaking down large units into a number of smaller units is often called 'decomposition', while the process of assembling large units from smaller units is called 'synthesis'.

Normalisation is an example of what is called 'top-down' design. Using top-down design a single structure is broken down into multiple sub-units. Using normalisation, a single entity containing a large number of attributes can be broken down into multiple entities containing a smaller number of attributes. In contrast E-R modelling is an example of 'bottom-up' design. In bottom-up design a number of individual data items are assembled into meaningful structures called entities.

Normalisation can be used to ensure that the entities that are produced during data modelling are designed in the best possible way for modelling the information requirements of a system. However, normalisation does not provide techniques for determining the relationships between these entities. This can only be achieved by a thorough understanding of the data requirements of the system. Normalisation is a process that can be followed by rote (it is even possible to purchase software that can automate the process of normalisation), but this alone will not lead to a detailed understanding of the data requirements of a system or an organisation.

Each of the normal forms has a formal definition. In the sections that follow, this formal definition is presented first, followed by a discussion of its meaning and application.

First Normal Form

DEFINITION

An entity is said to be in First Normal Form if all attribute values are atomic.

This means that each column in a table should contain only one value, not multiple values such as a list. For example, in a contacts database you might decide to include a single attribute in a contact entity into which a list of the contacts' interests could be entered. Alternatively, in an application designed for an estate agent to match clients to properties, you may be inclined to include a single attribute to hold a list of the features that the client would like (for example, three bedrooms, semi-detached, large garden).

Why is a list of values in a single attribute such a problem? Suppose that a single column in the Castellan system was designed to hold a list of names of staff members who had enrolled on a course. It would be very difficult to search for an individual name since it could appear anywhere in the list. It would be even more difficult to compare or perform calculations using only one value from the list. To do this you would need to be able to find out where the value was in the list and then separate it from all the other values.

The technical term for this capability is 'referential integrity'.

Worse still, such a list would make it impossible to use the features of a database system to ensure the quality of the information that it holds. A database provides the capability to check the appropriateness of a value entered in a column in one table against values held in another column in another table. However, this is only possible if each column contains just a single value, not a list.

When a table contains a number of fields that will hold the same attribute, the collection of fields is called a 'repeating group'.

So how do we get around this problem? Some designs comply with the requirement that each individual column should contain only a single value by having several different attributes in the entity, each of which holds the same data item (with a different value). Sometimes repeating groups of fields such as these are easily spotted – the presence of fields that are numbered is usually a good indication of a repeating group. The sample Excel list introduced in Unit 2 contains such a repeating group for the course attendees.

Course number	Course title	Start date	Attendee1 name	Attendee1 dept	Attendee2 name	Attendee2 dept
IND1	Staff induction	27/03/1998	Neil Smith	Accounts	Dipak Patel	Marketing
FIR1	Fire safety	29/03/1998	Peter Brown	Accounts	Joshua Ndola	IT
ACC1	Introduction to Microsoft Access	24/04/1998	Jenny Wong	Desktop Services	Peter Brown	Accounts
IND1	Staff induction	15/04/1998	Hardeep Singh	Personnel	Paula Fisher	Accounts

Table 5.1 The Excel list currently used by Castellan to hold course attendance data

With a repeating group like this it would be almost as difficult to search for an individual attendee as it is in a list of items in a single column. You would also have to search in each of the fields to see if it contained the value that you were looking for. Nor would it be possible to enforce the integrity of the data using the facilities of a database product. For this reason the rule for First Normal Form not only prohibits the use of lists of values in a single column, but also repeating groups of columns in an entity.

The cause of the problem here is the fact that the entity actually holds information about two separate things. In addition to information about a course it also holds information about the attendance of individuals on those courses. Given that an entity should hold information about one thing, and one thing only, the real solution to the problem is to remove the repeating group from the entity by breaking it into two separate entities. In this example we must create one entity to hold information about the courses:

Course number	Start date	Course title
IND1	27/03/1998	Staff induction
FIR1	29/03/1998	Fire safety
ACC1	24/04/1998	Introduction to Microsoft Access
IND1	15/04/1998	Staff induction

Table 5.2 The Course entity formed by decomposing the original Excel list in Table 5.1

And a second entity to hold information about the course enrolments:

Course number	Start date	Attendee name	Attendee dept
IND1	27/03/1998	Neil Smith	Accounts
IND1	27/03/1998	Dipak Patel	Marketing
FIR1	29/03/1998	Peter Brown	Accounts
FIR1	29/03/1998	Joshua Ndola	IT
ACC1	24/04/1998	Jenny Wong	Desktop Services
ACC1	24/04/1998	Peter Brown	Accounts
IND1	15/04/1998	Hardeep Singh	Personnel
IND1	15/04/1998	Paula Fisher	Accounts

Table 5.3 The Course enrolment entity formed by decomposing the original Excel list in Table 5.1

The combination of Course number and Start date would uniquely identify each entry in the entity in table 5.1, which, for the moment, we can call Course. The second entity shown in table 5.2, which we can call Course enrolment, would be uniquely identified by the combination of Course number, Start date and Attendee name.

Recognising repeating groups

In our example the repeating group was easy to see. In other cases the repeating groups may be more difficult to spot. What if staff members were required to attend the same course every year? We might be tempted to create an entity to hold information for each staff member's attendance on the course, with a separate attribute to hold information about each year.

Course number	Attendee name	1996 Attendance	1997 Attendance	1998 Attendance
FIR1	Neil Smith	31/03/1996	12/04/1997	01/05/1998
FIR1	Hardeep Patel	21/11/1996	20/10/1997	
SAF	Jenny Wong	01/06/1996	12/06/1997	30/06/1998

Table 5.4 A repeating group used to store historical data.

This structure is completely inflexible. What happens when the year 1999 comes around? We could redesign the entity to add another column, but in a database application we would have to redesign all the forms and reports in the database as well. Alternatively, we could reuse the 1996 attendance attribute thereby losing the information it contains. We would also have to hope that whoever uses the table later realises that the name of the column is now meaningless, since it no longer contains 1996 data.

Neither of these options is really a good solution. The problem is caused by the fact that the year columns are really a repeating group. By using a more generic term for the column names (Year1, Year2, Year3), the existence of the repeating group becomes apparent.

The need to categorise records can also result in repeating groups. An entity to hold expense account information may be designed to hold the various categories of expense by including a column for each category, as follows.

Date	Description	Amount	Car	House	Phone	Travel
15/01/1998	Petrol	25.00	25.00			
17/01/1998	Electricity bill	43.44		43.44		
21/01/1998	Season ticket	101.97				101.97

Table 5.5 A repeating group used to classify data

In Table 5.5 by renaming the fields Expense type 1, Expense type 2 and Expense type 3 the existence of the repeating group becomes obvious.

This method is fine in a spreadsheet, but in a database it can cause a lot of difficulties. What happens if we need to add another category of expense? In a spreadsheet this is not really a problem – you can simply use another column at the end of the sheet. However, in a database it may require the table to be redesigned, as well as any forms and reports that use data from the table.

A key indicator that there is a problem with this particular table is the fact that in each row many of the fields have no value, even though the record is complete. A large number of empty columns in a complete record are a good sign that the design is not optimal. Again, by giving the attribute a more generic name we can see that we have a repeating group.

This entity would be better arranged as follows.

Date	Description	Amount	Expense type
15/01/1998	Petrol	25.00	Car
17/01/1998	Electricity bill	43.44	House
21/01/1998	Season ticket	101.97	Travel

Table 5.6 The repeating group can be eliminated by classifying the entries using data values, rather than embedding the classification in the attribute names

Arranged like this, the classification is held as a data value. If we need to add another expense type it is simple a matter of adding another value to the table. It does not require any modification to the database design at all. In addition, with this design we can ensure the integrity of the data in the database by validating the expense types entered in this table against values held in another table.

Second Normal Form

| DEFINITION | *An entity is said to be in Second Normal Form if it is in First Normal Form, and if every non-key attribute is functionally dependent on the unique identifier.* |

Functional dependency
is a technical term
derived from
mathematics

An attribute in an entity is functionally dependent on another attribute if we can determine the value of the second attribute by knowing the value of the first attribute. For example, if we know the name of a country we can determine the name of its capital city. We can therefore say that the capital city is functionally dependent on the country name. Similarly, if we know the Employee number of a member of staff we can determine his or her date of birth. There is a functional dependency between the Employee number, and his or her date of birth.

Course number	Start date	Course title
IND1	27/03/1998	Staff induction
FIR1	29/03/1998	Fire safety
ACC1	24/04/1998	Introduction to Microsoft Access
IND1	15/04/1998	Staff induction

Table 5.7 The Course entity is in First Normal Form, but not in Second Normal Form

What can we say about the Course entity shown above? If we know the identifier for a course, we can determine the name of the course. Therefore, the Course name attribute is functionally dependent on the Course number attribute. For the entity to be in Second Normal Form each non-key attribute has to be functionally dependent on the complete unique identifier. Note the use of the word complete. Second Normal Form is only an issue if a combination of attributes is used to uniquely identify the entity. If the entity is uniquely identified using a single attribute, the entity is automatically in Second Normal Form.

In fact, there is
something in the data
that gives us a clue.
Notice how the same
Course name Staff
induction is repeated in
more than one row. We
are unlikely to have two
separate courses with
the same name, so
something must be
wrong.

Is Course number the unique identifier for this Course entity? In fact it is not. We can see that the same Course number appears more than once in the table, and so we can determine that it is not a unique attribute. Only the combination of Course number and Start date can be used to uniquely identify each instance of this entity. Given that the Course number column on its own can be used to uniquely identify the course name, we can say that the course title attribute depends on an attribute that is only part of the unique identifier. Put another way, the course title attribute is not functionally dependent on the complete unique identifier. Therefore, this entity is not in Second Normal Form.

The problem here is partly the use of words. This entity does not just hold information about courses: it holds information about courses and when those courses are offered. These are actually separate concepts. As the entities exist at the moment, we could not hold information about a course until it was actually available (that is, we could not hold information about a course while it was being designed or prepared).

Once again the problem is caused by a single entity holding information about two different things. Again the solution is to break this single entity into two separate entities. The first entity will hold information about the course in general, the second will store information about each offering of the course at a particular time. This is the revised Course entity

Course number	Course title
IND1	Staff induction
FIR1	Fire safety
ACC1	Introduction to Microsoft Access

Table 5.8 The revised Course entity

This is the second entity, which we can call Course offering.

Course number	Start date
IND1	27/03/1998
FIR1	29/03/1998
ACC1	24/04/1998
IND1	15/04/1998

Table 5.9 The Course offering entity formed by decomposing the Course offering

The Course entity is uniquely identified by the Course number attribute. The Course offering entity is uniquely identified by the combination of Course number and Start date attributes.

As a result of breaking the entity into two we now have a way to store data that relates to the course in general although it is separate from the data that relates only to a particular offering of a course. For example, if a particular course always lasts for a particular length of time, we add an attribute called Duration to the Course entity to store this data. On the other hand, if the location where a course is held differs every time the course is offered, we would add a Location attribute to the Course offering entity to store this data.

Third Normal Form

DEFINITION

An entity is said to be in Third Normal Form if it is in Second Normal Form, and if all non-key attributes are mutually independent.

An attribute in an entity can be functionally dependent on the unique identifier, but may also be functionally dependent on another non-key attribute. For example, if the duration of a course was different each time it was offered, we may decide to add two attributes to the Course offering entity to hold the End date and Duration of the particular course offering.

Course number	Start date	End date	Duration
IND1	27/03/1998	28/03/1998	2
FIR1	29/03/1998	29/03/1998	1
ACC1	24/04/1998	27/04/1998	4
IND1	15/04/1998	17/04/1998	3

Table 5.10 The Course offering entity expanded to hold information about duration

Recall that this entity is uniquely identified by the Course number and Start date attributes. If we know the values for the Course number and Start date, we can determine the Duration. Therefore the Duration attribute is functionally dependent on the unique identifier. However, it is also dependent on the values in the Start date and End date attributes.

The problem here is that Duration is a derived value that could actually be calculated. There are two possible solutions here:

- we could remove the Duration attribute and calculate the value as required, or

- we could remove the End date attribute and calculate this value by adding the duration to the Start date.

As a general rule an entity should not contain any attributes that can be derived from values in other attributes.

Not all transitive dependencies are the result of included calculated attributes in an entity. The Course enrolment entity suffers from a similar problem.

Course number	Start date	Attendee name	Attendee dept
IND1	27/03/1998	Neil Smith	Accounts
IND1	27/03/1998	Dipak Patel	Marketing
FIR1	29/03/1998	Peter Brown	Accounts
FIR1	29/03/1998	Joshua Ndola	IT
ACC1	24/04/1998	Jenny Wong	Desktop Services
ACC1	24/04/1998	Peter Brown	Accounts
IND1	15/04/1998	Hardeep Singh	Personnel
IND1	15/04/1998	Paula Fisher	Accounts

Table 5.11 Transitive dependencies may be caused by holding redundant data in an attribute

If we know a staff member's name, we can determine his or her department. We can say, therefore, that the department attribute is functionally dependent on the staff member name attribute. However, the staff member name is not the unique identifier for this entity.

Once again the problem here is caused by the fact that the entity is being used to hold data about two different things. The entity is supposed to hold information about course enrolments, but is also being used to hold additional information about the person who is attending the course. This may be of interest, but it simply does not belong in this particular entity.

We can resolve this by decomposing this entity into two. The first entity holds information about the staff members.

Staff number	Last name	First name	Department
401	Smith	Neil	Accounts
402	Patel	Dipak	Marketing
343	Brown	Peter	Accounts
212	Ndola	Joshua	IT
333	Wong	Jenny	Desktop Services
403	Singh	Hardeep	Personnel
404	Fisher	Paula	Accounts

Table 5.12 The staff member entity

The second entity holds information about the course enrolments.

Course number	Start date	Staff number
IND1	27/03/1998	401
IND1	27/03/1998	402
FIR1	29/03/1998	343
FIR1	29/03/1998	212
ACC1	24/04/1998	333
ACC1	24/04/1998	343
IND1	15/04/1998	403
IND1	15/04/1998	404

Table 5.13 The Course enrolment entity no longer holds redundant data about the staff member

Since the staff member's name is unlikely to be unique (there is every chance that there will be two staff members with the same name), the Staff number attribute has been introduced to uniquely identify the Staff member entity. The name has also been decomposed into its separate components to enable searching and sorting by the last name. The Course enrolment entity is uniquely identified by the combination of Course number, Start date and Staff number.

Higher Normal Forms

Higher Normal Forms do exist. However, they are mainly of interest in academic circles rather than in the practical application of database design. You will find these normal forms discussed in more theoretical texts about database design.

If common sense is followed it is likely that if your entity definitions are in Third Normal Form, they will also conform to the Higher Normal Forms.

Choosing the most appropriate unique identifier

The more experienced you become at data modelling, the more likely it will be that the entities that you produce in an E-R diagram will be fully normalised.

At first glance the normalisation process can seem very complicated. The basic rule is to ensure that each entity in your logical design (or each table in your physical design) holds information about one thing, and one thing only. To ensure that this is the case, check that each attribute in each entity can be determined by the whole of the unique identifier (and by no other attribute).

The rules of normalisation depend so heavily on the attributes that make up the unique identifier. Therefore it is most important to choose the correct attributes to serve this purpose. The following points should be borne in mind when choosing the attributes to make up the unique identifier.

- It must be possible to use the value held in the unique identifier to uniquely identify every single instance of an entity. There must be no exceptions to this rule. For example, it must be possible to use an individual Employee number, identify every single member of staff in an Employees table, from the managing director down.

- Using the attribute chosen for the unique identifier, it should be possible to identify all possible instances of the entity, not just those that exist at a particular time. For example, at a particular point in time an organisation may not employ two staff members with the same date of birth. However, this would not make an appropriate unique identifier, since there is every chance that the organisation could employ a new staff member with the same birthday as an existing staff member.

- An attribute or combination of attributes in an entity can be used as the unique identifier if it will uniquely identify all possible instances of an entity within the system. It is not necessary to uniquely identify all possible instances of an entity in the entire world.

- The unique identifier should not contain any unnecessary attributes. Since an Employee number itself can be used to determine the values of all other attributes for a staff member, it is not necessary to include any other attributes (such as the employee's name) in the unique identifier.

- Each instance of the entity should only contain facts about that particular entity. This is achieved by ensuring that each entity only contains attributes that are determined by its unique identifier. If an attribute is determined by another attribute that is not part of the unique identifier, it belongs in another entity.

- Each entity should not contain attributes that can be derived from calculations performed on other attributes that do not make up the unique identifier.

- However, when you break an entity into its components it is essential to ensure that no information is lost. If you cannot derive the value in one attribute from the values held in other attributes, you should not delete the attribute.

Revision exercises

1. What problems can be caused by having a repeating group in an entity?

2. What is meant by the term 'functional dependency'?

3. Castellan's training department currently uses an Excel list to store information about the loans for training materials to other departments. The table below shows the arrangement of this list.

Dept ID	Dept name	Date of loan	Item1 title	Item1 copy no	Item1 type	Item2 title	Item2 copy no	Item2 type
IT	Information technology	27/09/1998	Access 7 Further skills	1	Book	Introduction to Windows	1	Video
ACC	Accounts	29/09/1998	Sage for Windows	1	Book	Decision Support in Excel	1	Multi-media
IT	Information technology	24/10/1998	Visual Basic Complete Course	2	Book	Introduction to Windows	2	Video
PSNL	Personnel	15/11/1998	Dealing with change	2	Video	Effective Leadership	2	Book

The columns labelled Item1 title, Item1 type and Item1 copy no are repeated six times in the spreadsheet. Normalise this structure to Third Normal Form. How does the arrangement of entities produced by normalisation compare to those produced by E-R modelling?

6 Creating the physical data model

What you will learn in this unit

This unit describes how the logical data model is converted to a physical data model that can be implemented using a particular database product. Since we will be using Microsoft Access to implement the database, the physical model reflects the requirements of a relational database.

At the end of this unit you should:

❏ understand how entities in an Entity-Relationship (E-R) model are converted to relations in a physical data model

❏ understand that it may be necessary to denormalise the design in order to obtain the best performance from the system

❏ understand issues that are specific to the implementation of a database design using Microsoft Access.

Why create a physical design?

Up to now we have been careful to ensure that the data model that we have created does not reflect the requirements of any particular method of implementation. For this reason it is called a logical data model. This has been done to ensure that the data model truly reflects the requirements of the organisation and is not biased by the need to use a particular storage method or product.

A decision may even be made to implement the requirements using manual methods, rather than a computer-based system.

Finally we have reached the stage when we need to select the product that we are going to use to implement the requirements. Of course, it is unlikely that you will have a completely free hand in this decision. Any new system may need to fit in with other systems that already exist, or use the software or equipment that is already in use in the organisation.

When it has been decided what method or product to use, you can convert the logical data model to a physical data model that reflects the implementation methods of the product. It is often the case that some changes need to be made to the design in order to make the most effective use of the particular product.

Producing a physical data model for a relational database

The E-R model and the relational model for database design are based on the same mathematical principles. As a result, converting a simple logical data model produced using E-R diagrams to a relational database design is straightforward. However, there are some decisions that need to be made (and documented) to produce the best physical design and implementation.

The column or combination of columns that uniquely identify each row in the table is called the Primary key.

A relational database is composed of basic units of data storage called tables. Each table contains one or more columns that contain the data values. Each table contains one or more rows. Each row in a table is uniquely identified by the value in one or more columns. Tables are related to each other using relationships.

The basic steps to convert an E-R model to a relational database design are as follows.

1. Each entity in the logical data model becomes a table in the physical data model. If you have used a singular noun to name the entity, you can use the plural form of the same noun to name the table. For example, an entity called Course is implemented as a table called Courses.

2. Each attribute of the entity becomes a column in the table that is created from the entity. The name of the attribute will become the name of the column. Column names that appear in more than one table (for example, there is likely to be an attribute called Description in several entities) should be qualified with the name of the entity (for example, the Description attribute in the Course entity becomes a column in the course table called CourseDescription).

3. The components of the unique identifier for the entity will become the components of the Primary key of the table.

Columns created in related tables for the purpose of creating relationships are known as 'Foreign keys'.

4. The relationships in the logical data model will become relationships in the physical data model. In a relational database, relationships are implemented by duplicating the columns that make up the Primary key of the table on the one side of the relationship in the related table. For example, a one-to-many relationship exists between Departments and Staff members. To implement this relationship the column used for the Primary key in the Department table (the DepartmentID column) is duplicated in the table on the many side of the relationship (the Staff members table). Figure 6.2 shows the same relationship in the physical model. Please note that the staff member table in Figure 6.2 now includes the DepartmentID column required to implement the relationship.

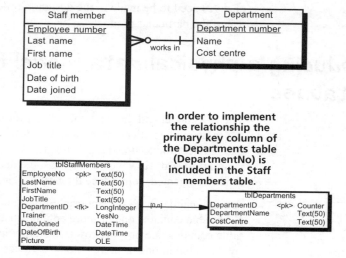

Fig 6.1
The relationship between Department and Staff member identified in the logical design

In order to implement the relationship the primary key column of the Departments table (DepartmentNo) is included in the Staff members table.

Fig 6.2
The implementation of the relationship in the physical design

Implementing an intersection entity

For more information about intersection entities, see Unit 4.

An intersection entity is an entity that is created to resolve a many-to-many relationship between two other entities. An intersection entity is implemented as a table in the database.

The primary key columns of the entities for which it is resolving the many-to-many relationship are duplicated in this entity as Foreign keys. At its most simple the table will contain only these columns. The combination of these columns forms the Primary key of this table.

A table created from an intersection entity in the logical data model may only contain the Primary key columns from the related tables

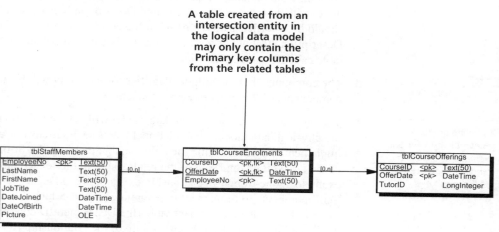

Fig 6.3
The implementation of the intersection entity in the physical design

Designing indexes

The physical design for a database may also indicate whether the individual columns in a table are to be indexed. An index is a construct in a database that can speed up searching for and sorting data. Indexing strategies are discussed in detail in Unit 16 on optimising database performance.

Denormalising the design

Denormalisation is the process of introducing intentional redundancy into tables to improve performance. This redundancy may involve storing data that could be derived by calculation, or by merging columns from two tables into a single table to avoid having to join them in a query.

The logical model for a system should always be fully normalised. The decision to denormalise should only be taken at the time of physical design.

Note the use of the word intentional in the paragraph above. Performance enhancement is often used as an excuse for poor database design. If you decide to denormalise part of the database design, this should be a conscious decision based on information that confirms that the current design is causing performance problems.

As with most design decisions, denormalisation involves trade-offs. Storing the results of a calculation in a table will certainly improve performance where it is necessary to aggregate the values in that column. However, you will have to create procedures in the applications that use the database in order to ensure that the calculated column is maintained when new rows are inserted or when the values are changed. You may also discover that while denormalising a table may make one type of retrieval more efficient, it could make others much more complicated and slower.

The following are common examples of denormalisation to improve performance:

- holding calculated values in parent tables
- holding calculated values in the same table
- merging tables.

Holding calculated values in parent tables

A common example of this sort of requirement is in an order processing system where the details of an order are stored in one table (order table) and the individual line items are stored in another table (order items table). Every time you want to process information regarding the total order value you must aggregate the appropriate columns in the two tables.

A common solution to this problem is to add a column to the order table that holds the total value of the order. (In fact you may want to have one column for the total value and another for the VAT total.) This will certainly make it faster to retrieve the total value of the order. However, you should consider the following additional work required to maintain this value.

- Every time a new line item is added to the order items table, the summary column in the orders table will need to be updated.

- Every time a line item is deleted from the order items table, the summary column in the orders table will need to be updated.

- Every time the extended price of a line item is changed in the order items table, the summary column in the orders table will need to be updated.

If the company's business rule states that an order cannot be changed after it has been accepted, this will not be too much of a problem. However, in other cases you may find that the performance of the system as a whole is compromised by the need to provide functions to perform this maintenance of the calculated value.

Denormalising the database design can lead to the same problems of inconsistent and incorrect data described in Unit 2.

As for implementing the functions to maintain the calculated column, we can achieve this sort of thing quite easily in Access when all data entry is guaranteed to take place through the use of a form. However, what happens if someone (more often than not the administrator of the system) goes into the tables directly to alter the quantity or price of a line item? The calculated field no longer holds the correct value, and any reports that use the field will show incorrect information.

Holding calculated values in the same table

Using the same example, is there a case for holding the extended price (quantity ordered multiplied by the item price) of each line item in the order items table? The only valid reason for doing this would be if we needed to make comparisons of this value against criteria (for example, if we needed to find orders that contained line items with an extended price greater than a certain value).

On the other hand, maintaining the data will take longer because whenever the data changes, the value will have to be calculated and written to the database. The problems of ensuring the validity of the calculated field if values are changed directly in the table as described in the previous section apply equally here.

Merging tables

When a row in a parent table is guaranteed always to have a fixed number of related rows in a child table, there may be an argument for merging the tables. For example, in a meteorological database we may want to hold figures for weekly rainfall. There will always be seven days in the week, therefore instead of holding information about the week as a whole in one table and the daily rainfall figures in another table, we could merge the two into a single table with a column for each of the seven days.

This arrangement is not in First Normal Form (because of the repeating group) but will make finding the average rainfall on a given day of the week much easier. Of course, it may make calculating weekly summaries less efficient (because the database will have to add across the row), which may lead you to consider holding yet another extra column for the weekly total.

This is one of the problems with denormalisation – once you start to denormalise you may find yourself on a slippery slope adding more and more calculated columns to your database tables to provide the required flexibility. But this flexibility is precisely the reason why we go through the process of normalisation in the first place.

Denormalisation can also increase the administrative burden of looking after a database. If you are worried that the values held in calculated columns may be incorrect, you will need to design and periodically run queries that check the integrity of the data held in the calculated columns. In most cases it is best to create the database based on the fully normalised data model. The design can be denormalised later if and when it becomes obvious that performance is inadequate and it has been established that denormalisation will effect the necessary improvement.

Other implementation issues specific to Microsoft Access

A Microsoft Access database can consist of a single file. This file can contain all the objects that implement the physical design of the database (the tables and the relationships), together with all the objects that make up the application interface that uses the database (queries, forms, reports, macros and modules). If the database is going to be used on a single machine, implementing the database as a single file may be a viable option.

The database file that contains the tables is usually referred to as the 'back end' and the file that contains the forms and reports is referred to as the 'front end'.

However, as soon as a database needs to be distributed to multiple users it is essential that the Access database be split into two separate files. One file contains the tables and relationships (and nothing else), while the other holds the application interface objects (and no shared data tables).

The reason for this is simple. In a perfect world we would design and implement our database, release it into production and never have to think about it again. In reality we will need to continue to work on the database, changing parts of the application while others are using it. If the database were implemented in a single file, distributing the objects that make up the revised version of the application would be extremely difficult. We cannot overwrite the existing file (since all the users' data would be lost in the process), so each application object would have to be imported into the existing file. In contrast, when the application objects are held in a separate file, this file can be overwritten at any time without loss of data.

If the database application is to be implemented on a network, you must also decide where the files are to be kept. If the data is to be shared by multiple users it is obvious that the 'back end' will have to reside on the network file server or in a peer-to-peer network on a shared drive. The choice is whether to store the 'front end' as a single shared file on the file server or to distribute a separate copy of the file on each user's local hard disk.

If you choose to store the 'front end' on the file server it will make the process of updating the application file much easier. However, this will result in an increase in network traffic because the application will have to be moved across the network as it is loaded into each workstation's memory each time it is run. If you choose to store 'front end' on the local hard disk the application will load much faster and there will be less network traffic. However, you will need to work out a strategy for distributing new versions of the application objects to each workstation each time there is a new release.

It is important to remember that although Access can be used as a multi-user database, locating the 'back end' database on a file server does not make it a 'client-server' system. A client-server database is (among other things) one in which the processing of the requests for data is handled by the server machine. For example, an application may make a request for a subset of data from a table in the database. In a client-server system the server processes the request and only returns the rows that match the request.

By contrast, in a 'file-server' database system such as Access, the server only processes the requests for data from a particular file. It is possible that all the rows in a table will be moved across the network to the workstation. The Access database that is resident in the workstation's memory processes the data returned by the file server. This database filters the data so that the rows actually required are presented to the user.

Revision exercises

1. Convert the logical data model created for the Castellan training materials database to a physical data model by completing the following tasks.

   (a) Choose the most appropriate names for the tables that will be created, and for each column in the tables.

   (b) Identify all the foreign key columns that will be required to implement the relationships in the logical data model.

2. Identify any areas of the design that might benefit from being denormalised. What changes would be required to the design? What implications would this have in terms of ensuring that all data was consistent and correct?

3. An Access database system stored on a file server is performing poorly. What are the factors that could lead to this poor performance?

7 Data design

What you will learn in this unit

This unit describes the various ways that can be used to represent data values in a database.

At the end of this unit you should:

☐ understand that the choice of a data type to represent a data value should be determined by the operations that will be performed on the data

☐ understand the problems that can be caused by missing values in a database

☐ understand how encoding schemes can be used to represent data values

☐ understand the different types of encoding schemes and the advantages and disadvantages of each.

Purpose of data design

The previous unit described methods to determine the overall structure of the database. This unit makes recommendations for the data types that you should use for the various data elements in the database and for schemes that you adopt for representing the data values in the database.

Choosing data types

A column in a table in a database has a number of properties that determine what can and cannot be stored in it, as well as what operations can and cannot be performed on the data. In any database system one of the requirements when defining a table is to specify the data type for each column.

The specific data types that are available in Microsoft Access will be presented in the next unit.

The particular data types that will be available will depend on the individual database product being used. What follows is a discussion of the general approaches you should take when deciding the data type for a column.

Determining the operations performed on data

Before deciding on the appropriate data type for the column it is necessary to determine the operations that will need to be performed on the data during its capture, processing and storage. Some processing operations can only be performed accurately if the data is stored in a particular way.

- **Will any mathematical operations be carried out on the data?** If this is the case, then the data should be represented as a number. You should remember that mathematical operations can only be carried out directly if two values use the same unit of measure. Bear in mind also that some numbers that need to be stored may actually represent a ratio or a percentage. Numbers that represent a ratio (such as an exchange rate, a speed expressed as miles or kilometres per hour, or an average) cannot be added together. However, a rate can be multiplied by a denominator to produce a new value. For example, a number of pounds sterling can be multiplied by an exchange rate to yield a new amount in another currency; a speed can be multiplied by a duration to yield the distance travelled.

- **Will the data be converted to another format?** Numeric data may need to be converted from one unit of measure to another. If this is the case then it must be stored in a form that makes this possible. The number of significant digits may also be an issue for the conversion to be accurate. Some conversion ratios are fixed (for example, inches to centimetres) while others vary over time (for example, the exchange rate for the pound to the French franc). Other data types may also need to be converted. Text data may need to be converted to another language or another encoding scheme.

- **Will any time calculations be performed?** A date can be subtracted from another date to yield a duration. A duration can be added to a date to yield another date. Two durations can be added together to yield another duration. It is necessary to understand that a time value that represents a point in time, and a time value that represents a duration are different concepts.

Numeric data

There are two types of data that involve numbers.

- **Numbers that represent a value.** Examples include balances in a bank account, the distance between two points and the number of people enrolled on a course. Any of these numbers may be the subject of a mathematical calculation.

- **Strings of digits.** Examples of these include telephone numbers, or bank account numbers in which the only valid characters are numbers. There will be no requirement to perform mathematical operations on this kind of data.

Numbers that represent a value

Numbers that represent a value should be defined using a numeric data type. Most database systems offer a number of different numeric data types that differ in their scale and precision. You must choose a data type whose scale is sufficient to hold the highest and lowest possible number that is a valid value for the column.

Many database products provide a specific money or currency data type for storing monetary values.

You should also choose a data type that allows the data to be represented to the required precision. If there is a requirement to hold decimal values, it is no good choosing a data type that only allows integers (whole numbers) to be stored. If the number that is being stored represents money values, it is no good choosing a data type that may lead to the loss of significant digits during calculations, and thus lead to rounding errors.

Strings of digits

Databases are often required to store numbers that do not represent a value. Since there is no requirement to perform mathematical calculations on the data, should these values be represented using a numeric data type or should they be represented as text?

If you choose a numeric data type, any leading zeros that form part of the string of digits will be lost. For example, the telephone number 0171 234 5678 will be stored as 1712345678, although a search for 01712345678 will find it. In some cases the leading zero may be significant. What if the numbers 123 and 0123 were both valid values in a column that requires uniqueness? If a numeric data type is used, the database would treat them as equal and disallow the second entry. In this case you must store the numbers using a text data type, not a number data type.

Different computer systems will sort numbers represented as text in different ways according to the character set used.

However, choosing a text data type brings its own problems. If we choose a text representation for a number, a query that sorts on this column will sort the numbers in the order of the computer representation of the characters, not their true numeric order.

If you sort on a series of numbers stored as text you will see a sequence such as 1, 10, 11, 2, 20, 21, 8, 9 and so on. You can avoid this problem by converting the text value to a number before sorting. Alternatively, you can explicitly format the text string with leading zeros, but this may lead to poor performance.

Another problem with the text representation of numbers occurs when searching for values against criteria. For example, if you were to search the sequence 1, 10, 11, 2, 20, 21, 8, 9 for values that are less than 30 (< "30"), you would get this result: 1,10,11,2,20,21. What happened to 8 and 9? These characters come after 30 in the machine collating sequence for characters representing digits, and are therefore excluded by the criteria.

So what is the best choice? If sorting and filtering according to a purely numeric sequence is important, and leading zeros are not significant, then a numeric representation is probably best. If sorting and filtering a range of values are not important (how often do you need to sort telephone numbers?), or if leading zeros are significant, a text representation is the most appropriate.

Text values

The data type used to store text values will depend on the number of characters that need to be stored. Most databases have a data type that is used to store variable length text strings, but they impose a limit on the size of these columns. In Access this is quite small (only 255 characters). What if you want to store more data? You could split the data up over several columns, but you would have to search each of these when looking for a particular value, and so this approach is not recommended.

In Access you can opt for a memo data type, which will store up to 64,000 characters. The problem is you cannot index a column that uses a memo data type, so searching for data will be slow. Even when Access finds the data it can only indicate the record that holds the data; it will not select the individual data value searched for in the column itself.

Dates

Microsoft Access uses a single data type to represent both dates and times.

Most databases (Access included) provide a specific data type for representing dates and times. In most database products dates are represented internally as a number. Access represents dates as the number of days that have elapsed since 31 December 1899. However, dates can be formatted for output in many different ways. If you specify a date but not a time, midnight is assumed by default. If you specify a time but not a date, 30 December 1899 is assumed. This can sometimes lead to interesting surprises.

Logical values

A proper logical value can only contain one of two values (True or False). Any data item that can be represented by one of two values (True or False, Yes or No), can be represented as a logical value. A numeric or text column that is limited to only two values could be used to represent a logical value. Some database systems (Access included) provide a specific data type for logical values that may require less storage that an ordinary numeric data type. However, by default this data type can actually store one of three values – True, False and Null.

Unit 8 shows how you can disallow Nulls in any column in a table.

The next section discusses Nulls in detail, but for now suffice to say that Null represents a missing or unknown value. This three valued logic can lead to a lot of problems. To avoid them you can require the database to disallow Null values in any column, but there are times when unknown will be a valid value.

Null values

A Null is used in a database to represent a missing or unknown value. For example, suppose we have a table that holds data about bank accounts with a column in the table to hold the gender of the bank account holder. A Null value in this column could mean that we did not know the gender of the account holder. However, it could also mean that a corporate body (such as a company or a club) held the account so the column was not appropriate in this case. In fact a Null can be interpreted in many different ways. It can mean (among other things):

- unknown

- unspecified

- not applicable

- currently unknown (but will be updated at a later date)

- was previously specified, but is now no longer required.

There are times when a Null value in a column can be used to tell us some specific information. A table that holds information about people could include a column to hold the date that the person died. If this column held a Null value we could infer that the person was still alive. However, there may be some instances where we know that someone is dead, but we do not know the date of their death. We could avoid a Null value by using an unlikely value to represent this information. But what happens if we needed to hold information about someone who did actually die on the date that we have chosen as the value to represent an unknown date of death? What if we want to use this column to calculate someone's age when they died?

Consequences of allowing Null values

There are various potential consequences that can occur where Null values are allowed.

- Because a Null can be interpreted in many different ways, a database will not treat one Null as being equivalent to another Null. This can be important when comparing values in different columns or when searching for values in more than one table.

- Not only is one Null not equal to another Null, Null is also not considered to be equal to any other value. As a result, multiple searches that may be expected to return all the rows in a table may not do so. For example, if you searched a table for all rows where the value in a column is equal to a particular value you would see one set of records. If you then searched the table for all the rows that were not equal to that value you might expect to see all the other records. In fact, you may not see the complete set of rows – the missing records will be those that have Nulls in that column.

- Null values propagate in calculations. If you perform a mathematical calculation involving a Null value, the result of the calculation will itself be Null. This makes sense – two times unknown can only be unknown. Please note that this is quite different to calculations involving zero – two times zero is zero.

Queries that can create Null values are discussed in Unit 11.

- Null is not equivalent to zero or to an empty character string. These are both valid values, while Null is a token that represents a missing value.

Even if you do not allow Nulls in the actual data values, it is possible for certain queries to return columns that contain Nulls.

Ways around Null values

If you think that Null values will cause you problems, then you may consider creating an encoding system where actual values are used to represent unknown or missing items. You may even be able to find encoding systems that already exist for the data item in question. For example, an International Standards Organization (ISO) standard exists for encoding valid values to represent gender:

0 = Unknown

1 = Male

2 = Female

3 = Not applicable

However, there is a problem with this arrangement. If we want to retrieve all records that are applicable we have to search specifically for all the applicable values. Alternatively, we must know what all the non-applicable values are and exclude them. If Nulls were used you could do a simple search for values that are not Null.

The use of an encoding scheme brings with it a number of other issues.

Data encoding schemes

The way that the data is represented in a database can be just as important as the design of the structure of the database. Unless you have been living on a desert island for the last five years you will have heard the phrase 'millennium bug' or 'millennium time bomb' used. One of the main causes of this particular problem is the poor choice made in the representation of dates inside computer systems.

In the early days of computing storage space was at a premium and every attempt was made to make data storage as compact as possible. For this reason, most early systems represented dates using two digits for the year (1970 was represented using the last two digits). In many systems the century was simply assumed to be the twentieth century. It was also assumed that a larger year value followed a smaller year value for sequencing purposes.

With the turn of the century now imminent, these assumptions no longer hold true and many systems need substantial changes to continue to work correctly. Worse still, some systems will cease working in 1999. Why? Because the encoding scheme used a value of 99 in the year to represent infinity, or a value that would never expire.

Qualities of a good encoding scheme

With hindsight we can see that the encoding scheme used for dates in these systems was not the best choice. But how can you avoid the same problem in your design? There are a number of objective criteria that we can use to assess the appropriateness of an encoding scheme in a database, including whether it is:

- complete
- unambiguous
- not error prone
- expandable
- a single concept
- consistent
- convenient
- verifiable
- well documented.

Complete

A good encoding scheme provides for all possible values to be represented. Since Nulls can cause so many problems, the encoding scheme should also avoid 'missing' values wherever possible. Rather than leave a column empty, the encoding scheme should provide separate values that mean Unknown and Not Applicable, if these values are valid for the attribute under consideration.

Unambiguous

There should be no possibility that a single value in the encoding scheme could mean more than one thing. Part of the year 2000 problem is the fact that the value 00 for a year could mean either 1900 or 2000.

Not error prone

When a code consists of an arbitrary sequence of letters or digits, it is easy to miss one or transpose two digits. Although the computer system can provide processing logic to detect some of these errors, a good encoding scheme attempts to avoid them. This can be achieved by breaking numeric codes into chunks (this is the case with telephone numbers, which in the United Kingdom are usually broken up into three groups of digits).

Expandable

The encoding scheme should allow for more values than currently required. A single character alphabetic code allows for 26 possible values. These may seem sufficient at the time that a system is designed, but many costly problems have occurred in other systems that made the same assumption.

Modern database systems provide a means to expand the size of a column in a table quite easily. However, you should consider that you might also need to change reports, screen forms and interfaces to other systems as a result of change to a table.

A single concept

Some existing codes embed several different meanings within the encoding scheme. This is often seen in accounting systems where part of an account code may represent the department, another part may represent a level in the chart of accounts, and another part represent the actual account.

This type of scheme can cause several problems in a database system and it would be better if each part was stored as separate codes. The database should provide the means to reassemble the entire code for presentation to the user in the form to which they are accustomed.

Consistent

A good encoding scheme is consistent in terms of any implied or embedded information. For example, a code for sizes might imply a unit of measurement or a scale being used. If a column holding codes for shoe sizes implies that the UK sizes are being stored, then that scale should be used consistently. If a code implies that millimetres are the unit of measurement being used, it should also be used consistently.

Imagine the confusion if an encoding scheme used millimetres for some values and centimetres for others. You could avoid this sort of problem by including an additional column that held the unit of measurement. However, the processing logic to deal with this inevitably will be complicated.

Convenient

Just as it is possible to choose an encoding scheme that does not allow for expansion, it is possible to go too far the other way. An encoding scheme that uses 10 digit codes where three would be sufficient is inconvenient and may lead to errors.

Users will quickly revert to an old manual system if the computerised system designed to replace it is inconvenient and error prone.

Verifiable

As we will see later, simple codes can be verified using some of the integrity rules provided by a database product. Many of the more complicated encoding schemes in use today provide a more thorough means of verifying their accuracy.

Some schemes employ error-detecting codes in which part of the code is used to verify the rest. The most common example of this is the use of a check digit, which is calculated from the value and position of the other digits in the code. Other schemes employ error-correcting schemes that can be used not only to detect errors, but correct them as well.

Well documented

Where codes are used it is important to ensure that the meaning of the code is well documented. In a database system, the codes and the meanings for the codes should be stored in the database itself. Modern database systems provide ways to translate codes 'on the fly' so that the user is presented with the meaning rather than the code.

> Don't avoid an existing encoding scheme simply because it was 'not invented here'.

Wherever possible you should use an existing encoding scheme. Nobody in their right mind would dream of inventing a new system for classifying demographic data when the postcode will fit the bill in most cases. However, it is common for organisations to invent their own encoding scheme when an existing scheme would do just as well.

The government is a good source of encoding schemes. Some are particular to this country while others are derived from international organisations such as ISO, the United Nations, the International Labour Organization and so on.

Types of encoding schemes

If you cannot find an existing encoding scheme to meet your requirements you may have to create one. There are a number of standard types of encoding scheme:

- arbitrary codes
- abbreviations
- enumerations
- scales
- hierarchies
- vectors.

Arbitrary codes

An arbitrary encoding scheme assigns an arbitrary value, usually a number, to the item to be encoded. In modern databases this is becoming more and more common, partly because the value can be assigned by the database and is guaranteed to be unique. It is also preferred because modern database applications are able to present the user with the translation of the code rather than the code itself (which is meaningless).

The biggest problem with this type of encoding scheme is duplicate values. It is extremely easy to allocate different codes for the same item. Since the code itself means nothing, it is not easy to spot different codes being used to represent the same thing.

Abbreviations

If you see a data entry operator's work area surrounded by 'cheat sheets' that are used to translate arbitrary codes, it is a sure sign of a less than useful encoding scheme.

Abbreviations are the most common form of codes in legacy systems where space was at a premium. Many abbreviated codes exist in the real world. The United Kingdom postal system uses a postcode system in which the first one or two letters represent the town where the main sorting office is located. While abbreviations may seem attractive, they can lead to problems. The sheer volume of codes can make them unworkable.

Enumerations

An enumeration encoding system uses numeric values according to some particular order. The order may be based on chronology (what happens first in time comes before what happens next in time), on a procedural order – (what happens first in the process comes before what happens next in the process).

The main problem with this type of encoding system is that if the order changes, or if new values need to be inserted in the middle of the list of values, the codes become arbitrary.

Scales

Scale encoding uses an implied unit of measurement such as metres, kilogrammes or volts. Obviously, the scale chosen has to be appropriate to the thing being measured (volts would not be an appropriate unit of measure for a code measuring liquids). Less obviously, the choice of a scale can affect the values being stored (metres may not be the best scale for a column storing tolerances on scientific equipment).

The requirement to convert from one scale to another may need careful consideration. Scales can only be converted from one unit of measure to another if they are the same type and measure the same attribute. The accuracy of the conversion can be affected by the precision of the values held. This will be an issue when making existing systems compliant with the rules for European Monetary Union. These rules mandate that conversion between currencies shall be accurate to six significant decimal figures.

Hierarchies

A hierarchy partitions values into categories, then sub-categories and so forth until a final level is reached. Hierarchies are usually represented graphically as a tree structure (such as an organisation chart). Examples of such hierarchies in the business world include charts of accounts and bills of materials.

Accounting systems may also use a range of values to organise the sections of a chart of accounts into a hierachy.

The Dewey decimal system is an example of a hierarchical encoding scheme. Different subject areas are allocated a series of numbers; the 500 series covers natural sciences and the series which begins with 510 covers mathematics – 512 covers algebra in particular. Such schemes tend to become inflexible as the distribution of values may change over time.

Vectors

A vector is made up of a fixed number of components. These components can be of fixed or variable length and can be ordered or unordered.

The most common example of a vector is a date, which consists of a component that represents the day, another for the month and a third for the year. The separation of the components is usually indicated by punctuation, which may differ according to the representation. For example, the slash character is the separator when a date is represented as 11/1/98, but the hyphen is used when represented as 11-Jan-1998. The position of the parts is determined by convention – in the UK we expect day/month/year; in the United States people expect month/day/year. The International Standards Organization has standardised on year/month/day.

You can see why dates can cause so many problems in a computer system, and why most software store dates as a numeric value that represents the number of days that have elapsed since (or before) a particular point in time.

These types of code are best avoided if possible. If it is not possible, try to store each part of the code separately and then reassemble the code for presentation purposes. The problem with this approach is the fact that it is possible to store individual values which, although valid in themselves, do not make up a valid combination of values.

Revision exercises

1. Choose an appropriate data type for the following data items:

    (a) ISBN number

    (b) price

    (c) purchase date

    (d) identifier for staff member's gender.

2. What type of encoding scheme is used in the following examples:

    (a) ISBN number

    (b) standard tyre sizes (for example, 165R14)

    (c) airport identification codes.

3. What are the main consequences of allowing Nulls in a database?

8 Implementing the database design using Microsoft Access

What you will learn in this unit

This unit describes how to implement the physical database design using the Microsoft Access product. At the end of this unit you should:

❑ understand how to create a new Access database

❑ understand how to create tables in the database

❑ understand how to define the fields in the table and set the data type for each field

❑ understand how to use field properties to implement business rules and other requirements

❑ understand how to create relationships between tables.

The objects that make up a database in Microsoft Access are stored in a file on the computer's hard disk. The first task when implementing the database design is to create the file that will hold the objects in the database.

Please note, it is not a good idea to use an Access database directly from a floppy disk. Access is a very disk-intensive program, and the poor speed of retrieval from a floppy disk will lead to a poor performing database. Worse still, the inability of a floppy disk to keep up with this intense activity may lead to corruption of the database file. You should always work with the database on the computer's hard disk and reserve the floppy disk for storing back-ups.

Creating the database file

To create a new database file, first start Microsoft Access. Now click on the File menu, and then choose the New database menu option. Access will display a dialogue giving you the option of creating a blank database or creating a database using the wizard.

Microsoft Access comes supplied with a number of wizards that can generate the objects that make up certain commonly used types of databases based on the answers that you supply to a number of questions. The wizards are useful if you want to create a database quickly without necessarily understanding the process that is involved. However, without this understanding it is not possible to change the design of the database if it is not exactly what you require.

Choose the blank database option. This dialogue will be displayed:

Choose the folder in which to store the file here

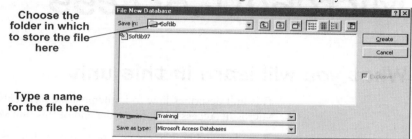

Type a name for the file here

Fig 8.1
Creating a new file to hold a Microsoft Access database

When you create a new blank database file it contains no objects at all. If you click on each of the tabs in the database window you will see no objects listed.

Each tab in the database window will ultimately display a different list of objects in the database

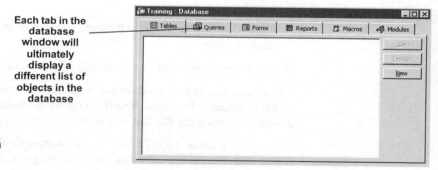

Fig 8.2
The database window. A new database may contain no objects at all

In order to store data in your database, you must first create the necessary tables.

Creating a new table

To create a new table, click on the Tables tab in the database window to ensure that it is the active tab. Now click on the button labelled New on the right-hand side of the database window. The following dialogue will appear.

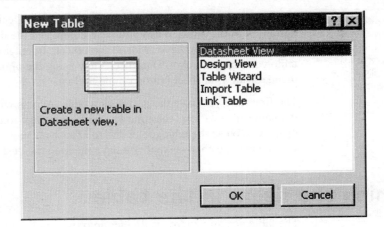

Fig 8.3
The create New
Table dialogue

Access also provides a number of wizards for creating individual tables, but we will create the tables without the assistance of the wizards. You can define the columns in your table by typing the column names in the first row of a grid, just like creating a list in Excel. This is called Datasheet View. However, it is not easy to see all the fields that you have defined in the table.

A better option is to choose to create the table design using Design View. Select Design View from the list, then click on the OK button. The table design window will be displayed.

This part of the window contains a grid. Each row in the grid is used to define a field in the table

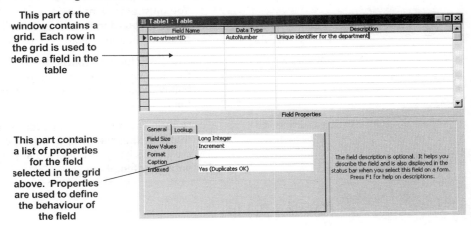

This part contains a list of properties for the field selected in the grid above. Properties are used to define the behaviour of the field

Fig 8.4
The table
design window

What is Design View?

Access provides at least two views of every object in a database. Design View is used to create the definition of the object, or to alter the design of the object. You cannot enter or change data in the database when you are in Design View. To add, delete or update records in the table itself, you must first switch to Datasheet View.

If you close the Table Design View window without saving your design, Access will automatically prompt you to save the changes.

When you are working with table objects, you use Design View to create the definition of the table. When you have completed the design you must save the changes that you have made to the object. To enter or change data in the table you must switch to Datasheet View using the option on the View menu, or the Datasheet button on the toolbar.

The first time you save the design of a table, Access will prompt you to give it a name. Thereafter, each time you make a change to the design of the table then try to close the table, or switch to Datasheet View, Access will prompt you to save the changes that you have made to the design.

Defining the fields in the table

The table design window is divided into two parts. The top part contains a grid that allows you to define each column in the table. Confusingly, each row in the grid becomes a column in the table when viewed as a Datasheet. Access refers to the columns in a table as fields. The grid contains three columns in which you can specify the following information.

Column name	Meaning
Field name	Type the name of each field that you want your table to contain in a separate row. For example, the Department table would need a separate field for the Department ID name and date of birth. You must enter a name for each field that you require. You cannot have two fields with the same name in the same table.
Data type	Use this column to specify the type of data that the field will contain (for more information, see below). You must specify a data type for each field.
Description	Use this column to type in additional information that describes the field, or the type of data that the field is likely to hold. You are not required to enter anything here.

Naming fields

In an Access database field names can be up to 64 characters long and can contain spaces. You can therefore choose meaningful names for each field without the need to resort to abbreviations.

Although you can use spaces in the field names, it is a good idea not to. When a field name contains spaces, Access will need some way to indicate what is the beginning and end of a field name when referring to the field in other places. To do this Access uses square brackets. For example, if you had a field called Last Name, Access would refer to the field as [Last Name] to avoid confusion. In most cases Access does this automatically, but sometimes it may not get it right, which can lead to errors.

It is also not a good idea to use punctuation characters in your field names. It may be the case that the size or usage of the system may grow beyond the capabilities of Access. As a result it may have to be 'upsized' to a more powerful database product such as SQL-Server or Oracle. If your field names contain spaces or other punctuation characters (like £, $, & or *), this process will be made more difficult.

Choosing a data type

For more information about choosing the most appropriate data type for a field, see Unit 7.

The most appropriate data type for a field is determined not only by the type of data that the field will hold, but also by the ways in which the data will be used. Access offers the following data types from which you can choose.

Data type	Size	Used for
Text	Up to 255 characters	Any data that you want to hold as a sequence of characters. Names, addresses, titles and so on would all be stored as text. It is also a good idea to store numeric data such as telephone numbers and part numbers as text, since you will not be performing mathematical calculations on these numbers, storing them as text will make it easier to display the number in the required format.
Memo	Up to 64,000 characters	Any character data that is too long to hold in a text field.
Number	Up to 8 bytes	Any numerical values (except amounts of money) on which you intend to perform mathematical calculations.
Date/Time	8 bytes	A particular date or a particular point in time. Access stores dates internally as a number, not as text. The number represents the number of days that have elapsed since 31 December 1899.
Currency	8 bytes	Any monetary values. You should use this data type rather than a number because Access stores currency data types to a higher degree of precision in order to avoid rounding errors when performing calculations.
Auto number	4 bytes	A unique, but arbitrary number that Access assigns in sequence as each new record is created. Use to provide a Primary key field when no suitable values are available in the other fields in the table.

Yes/No	1 bit	Use this data type for fields that can contain one of two values such as True or False, Off or On, Yes or No. In fact this field can contain three possible values – True, False or Null, which represents a missing or unknown value.
OLE Object	Up to 1 gigabyte	Objects created by other applications such as bitmap pictures, sound files, movies or word processing documents.
Hyperlink	Up to 6144	Contains the path to an object, document or page on the World Wide Web, or another Internet address.
Auto Lookup wizard	N/A	Creates a field that will be used to implement a relationship. For more information, see the section entitled 'Creating a relationship using the Auto Lookup wizard' below.

Describing fields

The information in the description field of the table design is used for documentation purposes only – Access does not use this information itself. You are not required to enter anything here, but it is a good idea to do so. If anyone else is going to work on your database it can make their job of understanding your design that much easier if each field has been given a meaningful description.

Setting field properties

You can think of a property as a setting, the value of which determines some aspect of the object's behaviour.

Each field in a table has a set of properties that can be used to define the storage space that is used, the range of allowable values that can be stored in the field, how the values in the field will appear when displayed and so on.

The bottom part of the table design window contains a text box for each property which is appropriate to the field that is selected in the top part of the window. As you select different fields in the top part of the window, you will see that the list of available properties in the bottom part of the window change. The list of available properties is determined by the field's data type.

Please note, before setting field properties you must ensure that the appropriate field is selected in the grid in the top part of the window. If you fail to do this you may find yourself setting properties for the wrong field.

In many cases a property can be set to an expression. An expression can be a literal value, an instruction to the computer to perform a calculation or a

Expressions are discussed in detail in Appendix A.

function that is built into the Access product. An expression is similar to a formula in a spreadsheet product such as Excel.

Field size property

The field size property determines the maximum length of data that can be stored in a text field, or the precision and scale of a number field. For a text field this property holds a number that represents the number of characters that the field can hold. By default, this value is set to 50 characters. The maximum value allowed is 255 characters.

Please note, Access stores text data in variable length fields. This means that even if you have set the field size property of a field to 255 characters, Access will only use as much space on the disk to hold the amount of data that has been entered. If only 10 characters have been entered in the field, Access will only use 10 bytes of storage on the disk to store that data.

For a number field, the field size property controls the range of values that can be held in the field (its scale) and to what level of accuracy those values will be stored (its precision). The following values are available for setting the field size property of a field using the number data type.

Setting	Range of values	Decimal places	Space used	Used for
Byte	0 to 255	None	1 byte	Very small whole numbers (no decimals)
Integer	−32,768 to 32,767	None	2 bytes	Small whole numbers
Long Integer	−2,147,483,648 to 2,147,483,647	None	4 bytes	Large whole numbers (also for Foreign keys to Auto numbers – see below)
Single	-3.4×10^{38} to 3.4×10^{38}	7	4 bytes	Small real numbers (including decimals)
Double	-1.797×10^{308} to 1.797×10^{308}	15	8 bytes	Large real numbers

Limiting the field size to the smallest value that is sufficient to your needs may increase performance in an Access database.

Format property

The format property allows you to specify how Access should display the data after it has been entered in a field. It is important to realise that this property does not affect how the data is stored in the table, only how it appears on the screen or on printed output.

Depending on the data type of the field, Access will show a list of commonly used formats for the field in the drop down list for the format property. For example, here is a list of the values that will be displayed for a Date/Time field.

General Date	19/06/94 17:34:23
Long Date	Sunday 19 June 1994
Medium Date	19-Jun-94
Short Date	19/06/94
Long Time	17:34:23
Medium Time	05:34 PM
Short Time	17:34

Fig 8.5
Choosing the display format for a field

Note display formats are also determined by the international settings defined in the Windows control panel.

You are not limited to these commonly used formats. Access provides a way of designing custom formats using format strings. For example, if you would like to display dates with a short day and month, but a year containing the century value you could enter 'dd/mm/yyyy' in the format property text box.

The format property can also be used to display meaningful values for fields whose data type has been set to Yes/No. For example, you may want to keep a record of an author's gender. The best way to do this would be to create a Yes/No field that indicates whether the author is male or female (the name of the field should make it clear what Yes means and what No means).

In a field called Female, where yes means that the author is female, you could set the format property of the field to the following: "Female","Male"

Access will display the word Female if the value held is True, and the word Male if it is False. However, when entering data you cannot type either the word Male or Female – Access will only accept True or False, Yes or No.

The possible formatting options offered by Access are too numerous to list here. For more information, read the format help topic. To do this, click on the format property field then press the F1 key on the keyboard.

Decimal places property

The Decimal places property works with the format property to control how many decimal places are visible when the data in the field is displayed. It does not alter the precision of the data that is stored in the table, only the value that is displayed.

Input mask property

An input mask provides a visual guide to a user when entering data into a field. By using an input mask you can display characters that act as place holders indicating where data has to be entered. You can also display literal characters that will be displayed on the screen, but will not be stored with the data in the field.

An input mask can be used to restrict individual characters in a field to a predefined range of values. In addition, you can prevent confidential data from being displayed on the screen while being entered by using a password input mask.

You can require that a date is entered in dd/mm/yyyy format by specifying an input mask like this: 99/99/0000;0;_

This mask will prompt for data in this format.

Fig 8.6
An input mask provides guidance when entering data from MS Word

Access provides context sensitive help for all properties in this way.

When the field contains no data the input mask displays guides for data entry

The possible input mask options offered by Access are too numerous to list here. For more information read the input mask help topic. To do this, click on the input mask property field and then press the F1 key on the keyboard.

Problems with input masks

Input masks work well if the user uses the keyboard navigation techniques to move to a form. If, however, the user uses the mouse to click on the field the insertion point may end up in the middle of the input mask. As a result the user may run out of room in the mask and not be able to enter a valid value.

Caption property

The caption property controls what is displayed in the column heading for a field when viewing a table as a datasheet. If you have chosen to follow the advice given earlier and create file names without any space, this property can be used to display user-friendly field names (including spaces).

Default value property

A default value is a value that is automatically entered in a field if no other value is specified. You can use this property to speed up data entry by specifying a value that is used often. For example, if you were creating a customer database, and the majority of your customers are in Birmingham, you could specify this as the default value for a town field.

You can also use this property to set values for fields of which the user may be unaware. For example, in an order processing system you may want to keep track of the status of an order. You could include a current status field in the order table and assign a default value of 'received' to this field. When the record is created, Access will automatically allocate this initial status to the record.

For more information about the functions that are available in Access, see Appendix A.

You can also use some of the built-in functions that Access provides in this property. If you wanted to know when each record in a table was created, you could create a field to hold this data and assign a default value of Date(). This is a function that adds the current date (as indicated by the computer's internal clock).

Validation rule property

Setting a field's data type goes some way to restricting the set of values that can be entered into the field. By setting the validation rule property you can further restrict the values that Access will allow to be entered.

Some validation rules are usually based on the business rules of an organisation, while others may be just common sense. For example, if the company has three branches, we might want to restrict values in a field that stores the name of the branch where each course takes place to one of the three branch names. We could do this by entering the three values like this:

"North" Or "South" Or "West"

For a longer list we could save typing by entering the values like this:

In ("North", "South", "West")

Please note, this technique is reasonable for a list of up to six values. Beyond this, it may be wise to create a separate table in the database to hold these values and validate the data by means of a relationship. This is especially true if the values in the list are likely to change at some point in the future.

Some validation rules may involve comparisons. If you do not want a currency field to hold negative values, you can set a validation rule of >=0. Access will ensure that any value entered will be greater than or equal to zero.

Validation text property

When a validation rule is broken, Access will display by default a very unfriendly error message. The validation text property allows you to create a much more specific message. Type the text of the message that you want to be displayed in this property.

Required property

A Null value indicates that the value is missing or unknown. See Unit 7 for more information about Nulls.

You can use the required property to specify that the field must contain a value for every record in the table. If a value has not been entered in a field whose required property has been set to True, Access will display an error message and the record will not be saved.

If the required property is set to False and the user does not enter a value into the field, its value will be set to Null.

Allow zero length property

It is possible for text or memo fields to store zero length strings. A zero length string is a data value that is stored as a string of characters, but which, in fact, contains no characters at all. A field that contains a zero length string may behave differently to a field that holds Null, although they both look the same (they are both blank).

By default Access does not store zero length strings, but setting this property to True will allow zero length strings to be entered.

Indexed property

An index is a construct in a database that can speed up searching for and sorting data. Indexes are discussed in detail in Unit 16 when we look at optimising the performance of the database.

Setting the Primary key

The Primary key is used to uniquely identify each row in the table.

Once you have created the field (or fields) that will act as the Primary key for the table, you can define it as such in the table design. To set the Primary key for the table, do the following.

1. Select the field by clicking on the grey row selector button to the left of the row. If the Primary key consists of more than one field you will need to select all the rows by dragging over the row selector buttons for all of the fields involved.

Click on the row selector button for the field that will be the Primary key

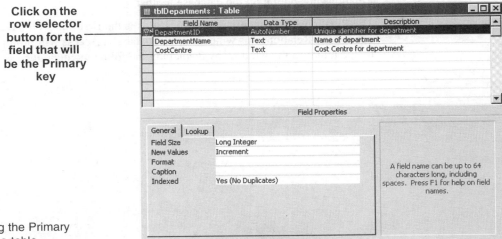

Fig 8.7
Defining the Primary key for a table

2. Set the Primary key either by clicking on the Edit menu and choosing Set Primary Key, or by clicking the button with the key symbol on the table design toolbar. When the Primary key has been set you should see a small key icon in the row selector button.

Creating Foreign key fields

You create the fields that will act as Foreign keys in the same way as any other field. However, there are some rules that you must follow when creating Foreign keys.

In most cases the Foreign key field must be the same data type as the Primary key field in the table to which it is related. The exception to this is when the related Primary key is an Auto number field. A Foreign key that is related to a Primary key that is also an Auto number must have its data type set to number, and the field size property set to Long Integer.

For more information about Foreign keys, see Unit 6.

There is no requirement for a Foreign key field to have the same name as the Primary key to which it relates, but this can make the database design easier for others to understand.

Creating relationships

Once you have created the tables that form both ends of a relationship you can create the relationship between them. It is best to do this when both tables are empty because Access may not be able to fully implement the rules that apply to a relationship if any data that is already in the table violates the rules.

Relationships are defined in the database using the Relationships window. To view the Relationships window, first select the database window then either click on the Edit menu and choose Relationships, or click on the Relationships button on the database toolbar.

The Relationships window will open. If this is the first time you have opened the Relationships window in this database, Access will prompt you to add tables to the window by displaying the following dialogue.

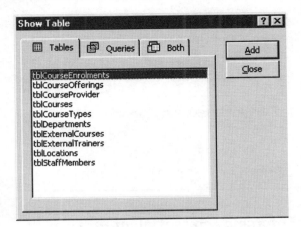

Fig 8.8
Selecting the tables
to show in the
Relationships

If this dialogue does not appear automatically, you can display it either by
clicking on the Relationships menu and choosing Show table, or by clicking
on the Show table button on the Relationships toolbar.

To add tables to the Relationship window, select the table from the list of
available tables and then click on the Add button. Repeat for the other tables
for which you want to create or view relationships. When you have added all
the tables you want to see, click on the Close button.

Tables are represented in the Relationships window as a rectangle containing
a list of all the fields in the table. The Primary key field or fields are shown
in the list in bold type. You can rearrange the Relationships window by
dragging on the box that contains the table's name at the top of the rectangle.

**Each box in the
Relationships
window
represents a
table in the
database**

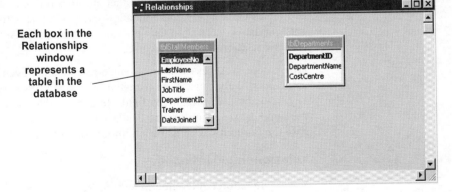

Fig 8.9
The relationships
window

To create a relationship between two tables, click on the Primary key field
concerned then drag it over to the related table and drop it on the Foreign
key field. You will see the following dialogue box appear.

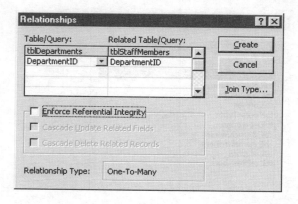

Fig 8.10
Defining a relationship

Enforcing referential integrity

Referential integrity is
used in a database like
Access to implement an
existence dependency
identified in the logical
data model. For more
information about
existence dependencies,
see the section on
relationships in Unit 4.

If you click on the Enforce Referential Integrity option, Access will ensure
that any value that is entered in the Foreign key already exists in the Primary
key field of the related table. Enforcing referential integrity is an excellent
way of ensuring the quality of data that is entered into the related table.

For example, in an order processing system you can ensure that it is not
possible to enter an order for a customer that does not exist by enforcing
referential integrity between an Orders table and a Customer table. In the
Courses database, the creation of records for course attendances for non-
existent staff members is prevented by enforcing referential integrity on the
relationship between the Staff member table and the Course attendance
table.

If you try to create a relationship that enforces referential integrity between
two tables that already contain data, Access will check to ensure that the
existing data conforms to the new rule. If it does not, Access will not permit
the new relationship to be created.

Please note, if Access will not create a relationship, even if the tables are
empty, the likely cause is a mismatch of the data types between the Primary
key field and the Foreign key field. Remember that the two fields must be
the same data type, unless the Primary key field is an Auto number. In this
case the Foreign key must be a number with a Long Integer data type.

Relationship cardinality

For more information
about the cardinality of
relationships see
Unit 4.

When you enforce referential integrity, Access needs to know whether this is
a one-to-one relationship, or a one-to-many relationship. This is called the
'cardinality' of the relationship.

Cascading updates and deletes

When you enforce referential integrity, Access will prevent you from
deleting a record on the Primary key side of the relationship if any related
records exist in the other table. If you were allowed to delete these records it
would leave 'orphaned' records in the other table. This makes good sense – if

you could delete a customer record when related orders still exist in the database, there would be little point in insisting that the customer record existed before the order records were created.

If the box labelled 'Cascade delete related records' is checked, Access will allow you to delete the record on the Primary key side. It will also delete every related record in the table on the other side of the relationship with very little warning.

If you check the box labelled 'Cascade update related fields', Access will automatically update the values in the Foreign key field in the related table whenever you change the Primary key field in the relationship.

Checking this box will have no effect if the Primary key field has an Auto number data type - you cannot update Auto number fields, so the value will never change. However, if the Primary key is another data type, this option can save a lot of work. For example, if code values are used as keys, imagine the work that would be involved in finding and updating the values in related records.

Choosing to cascade deletes can lead to unexpected loss of data. You should consider carefully the consequences of clicking on this box.

Editing an existing relationship

To edit the characteristics of an existing relationship, open the Relationships window, then click on the line that represents the relationship you want to edit. Now double-click on the middle of the line. Access will display the Relationships dialogue box.

Deleting a relationship

To delete a relationship, open the Relationships window and then click on the line that represents the relationship you want to delete. Now press the Delete key on the keyboard. Access will prompt you to confirm that you wish to delete the selected relationship.

Creating a relationship using the Auto Lookup wizard

A new feature of Microsoft Access 97 is the Auto Lookup wizard. This wizard automates the process of defining a Foreign key field in a related table and creating a relationship between the two tables. In addition, the wizard will define the lookup properties for the field so that Access can display other non-key values from the related table using a combo box or a list box.

For example, the Courses table requires the creation of a Foreign key to the Course types table. The Auto Lookup wizard will ask you to select the related table, then automatically create the Foreign key field with the correct data type. It will also ask you to select the column or columns that will be used for display purposes. Since the Primary key field of the Course type table is an Auto number, we can instruct the wizard to display a more meaningful value to the user (in this case the Course type description column).

There are two important points to note:

- When the wizard creates a relationship, it does not set any referential integrity constraints. If you require Access to enforce referential integrity between the two tables, you will have to open the Relationships window and edit the Relationship as described above.

- If the Foreign key value is related to an Auto number field, the wizard does not remove the value of zero that is automatically assigned to the Default value property of a number field. Since an Auto number field will never hold a value of zero, it is important that this Default value is deleted.

Modifying the design of a table

Microsoft Access is very flexible when it comes to changing the design of a table. However, you should be aware of some issues that arise when changing a table's design.

- If a field already contains data, you cannot change its data type to Auto number as this would mean that any existing data would be lost. If you need an Auto number field on a table that already contains data, you should add a completely new field to the table.

- If you change a field's data type or field size property to a smaller size or precision, you run the risk of losing data. For example, if you change a field from a Double to a Long Integer you will lose all record of any decimal values held in the field. Access will normally warn you when saving changes to a table if any precision of data will be lost.

- You cannot change a field's data type if the field forms part of a relationship between two tables. To get round this you must first delete the relationship, alter the data type of the fields concerned and then recreate the relationship.

- You cannot delete a table, if it is on the Primary key side of a relationship.

- If you add validation rules to a table, Access will check to ensure that the values that already exist in the table comply with the new rules. If any existing values do not comply with the rules, Access will not allow you to save the table design.

- When you make changes to a table, Access will not automatically amend other objects in the database that reference the table. For example, you may have created a form that is based on the table. If you delete a field from the table, Access will not automatically delete that field from the form. If you change the name of a field in the table you will find that the field on the form will no longer correctly display data. Instead you will probably see a #Name? error appear in the form field. A query based on the table may not run at all after the table has been changed.

The Castellan data model implemented in Microsoft Access

Figure 8.11 shows the Castellan data model implemented using Microsoft Access. If you compare this to the logical data model presented in Unit 4, (Figure 4.12) you will see how similar they are.

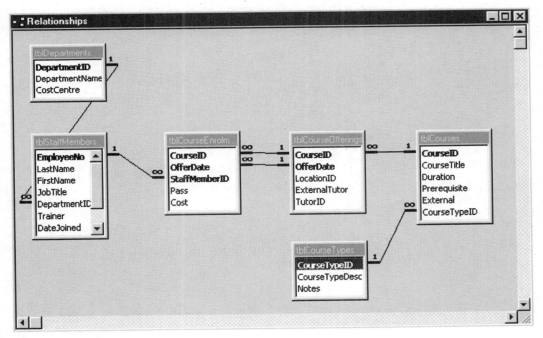

Fig 8.11 The Access implementation of the Castellan data model

Revision exercises

1. What is the purpose of the Description column in the table design window?

2. Which table property is used to specify a value that will be inserted if no other value is provided?

3. How can you ensure that a value is always entered in a particular column in a table?

4. What is the purpose of a Primary key?

5. What is the purpose of referential integrity? Give two examples of the use of referential integrity constraints.

9 Capturing data

What you will learn in this unit

This unit discusses some of the ways that you can get data into your database. At the end of this unit you should:

❐ understand the techniques for entering data into a table in a Microsoft Access database

❐ understand how to sort the rows in a table

❐ understand how to search for values in a table

❐ appreciate that if you are converting an existing computerised system you may have to do a considerable amount of work 'cleaning up' the data before you will be able to import it into your Access database

❐ understand the choices that are available for using data in an existing computerised system.

Preparing for data capture

Once you have created the tables that implement your database design you must begin the task of getting the data into the database. It is important to ensure that you have set up the relationships in the database, along with all other integrity constraints, before you start entering data. If you do not do this you will almost certainly encounter problems when trying to set up these constraints later. This is because the data that has already been entered may violate the constraints.

If you are automating an existing manual process you will have no choice but to enter the data manually. If you are converting from an existing computerised system you will need to find some way of exporting the data from that system and importing it directly into Access. Microsoft provides a number of ways to import data into Access. These are discussed in the second part of this unit.

Entering data directly into a table

Using Access it is possible to enter data values directly into a table. This is a viable option in the following circumstances:

• the volume of data to be entered is small

• the table only has a few columns.

In most cases you will want to use a form to enter data rather than a datasheet (forms are discussed in Unit 10). Nonetheless, there are important concepts that apply equally to the process of entering data into a table and entering data using a form.

As mentioned previously, there are two views of an Access table – Design View and Datasheet View. In Design View you can change the design of the table by adding or removing fields, setting properties and so on. In Datasheet View you can see the data values held in the table, add and delete rows, and update existing values.

Datasheets look very much like spreadsheets, so if you are familiar with a spreadsheet product such as Microsoft Excel you should not have too much trouble moving around in a datasheet. However, there are some important differences between the way that a datasheet saves data and the way that a spreadsheet saves data.

A datasheet is visually an arrangement of rows and columns. The figure below shows the main parts of a datasheet window.

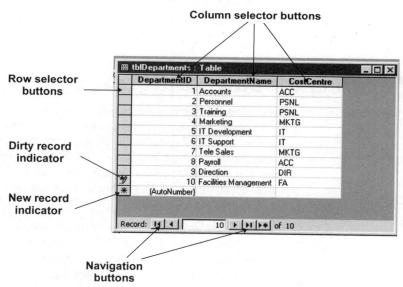

Fig 9.1
The parts of a
datasheet window

Creating a new record

Even when you open a table that contains no records, you will see a single empty row in the table. This is where you can type the values that will form

The row for a new record is indicated by the * symbol in the record selector button.

the new record. When you start typing in this row, Access automatically creates another empty row at the bottom of the datasheet. In a table that contains some data, the empty row for the new record will be at the bottom of the datasheet.

When you start typing values into a row in a datasheet, the symbol in the record selector button changes to a small pencil. This indicates that the record has been altered but not yet saved.

Saving the data

Access will automatically save changes that you make to a record.

The way that you save the data in a datasheet is very different to working with a spreadsheet. When you use a spreadsheet, the data that you enter into a sheet is only stored on the computer's disk storage when you explicitly save the file. A database on the other hand will automatically save data in a row that has changed whenever the following occur:

- you move off the row onto another row

- you close the datasheet window in which you have been working.

You can also explicitly save the changes made to a record without moving to another record by clicking on the Records menu and choosing Save record (or by holding down the Shift key and pressing Enter).

As Access saves the data every time you move off a record that has been changed, it can create a lot of disk activity. This is one of the reasons that it is not a good idea to work with an Access database that is stored on a floppy disk. Floppy disks cannot really cope with such continuous disk access.

Access automatically saves the changes that you make to the data in a table. It will not automatically save the changes that you make to the objects that you create in the database. For example, when you change the structure of a table in design mode you must explicitly save these changes by clicking on the File menu and choosing Save.

Moving around a datasheet

Only one cell in the datasheet grid can be active at any one time. The active cell receives the input from the keyboard. To be able to enter data into the correct cell in the datasheet you need to know how to move around.

You can use the mouse to select the required cell by clicking on it. However, when you are entering data, having to reach for the mouse can waste a lot of time. Instead, you can use the keyboard methods for moving around the datasheet.

To	Do this
Activate the cell in the next column	Press the Tab key
Activate the cell in the previous column	Hold down the Shift key and press the Tab key
Move down one row	Press the down arrow key
Move up one row	Press the up arrow key
Move down one window	Press the Page Down key
Move up one window	Press the Page Up key
Go to the first column in the first row	Hold down the Control key and press Home
Go to the last column in the last row	Hold down the Control key and press End

You can also navigate through the rows of a datasheet using the navigation buttons at the bottom of the datasheet window.

Moves to:

First record **Next record** **New record**

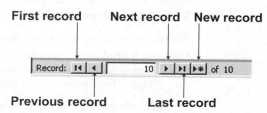

Previous record **Last record**

Fig 9.2
Navigation buttons on a datasheet window

The record number for a record will change as data is added to or deleted from a table.

You can move to a particular row in the datasheet by typing the row number in the white box between the navigation buttons. However, since the ordering of rows will change as you work with the table, this is not as useful as it might at first seem.

Using the secondary mouse button

Like most other Microsoft Windows 95 applications, Access provides the ability to select from a list of common commands on a shortcut menu that appears when you click using the secondary mouse button. Unless you have altered the default settings in Windows, the secondary mouse button is the right mouse button. Figure 9.3 shows the shortcut menu that appears when you right click on the row selector buttons in a datasheet window.

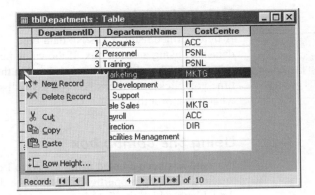

Fig 9.3
Navigating using the
secondary mouse
button

Entering and editing data

The values that you type using the keyboard are entered into the active cell
in the datasheet grid. When you enter a cell that already contains data, the
contents of the cell are selected. The default behaviour in Windows is for the
text that you type to replace the current selection. What this means in
practice is that anything you type will completely obliterate what was
already in the cell. This may not be what you intended.

If you want to edit the existing data you must press the F2 key to enter Edit
mode. This will place an insertion point (a blinking vertical bar) at the end
of the contents of the cell. Now that you are in Edit mode you can use the
standard Windows keystrokes to move the insertion point within the cell.

To	Do this
Move the insertion point to the beginning of the cell contents	Press the Home key
Move the insertion point to the end of the cell contents	Press the End key
Move the insertion point one character to the left	Press the left arrow key
Move the insertion point one character to the right	Press the right arrow key
Revert to selection mode	Press the F2 key again

You may have noticed that when you are in selection mode you can use the
left and right arrow keys to move the active cell one column to the left or
right. Although this does work, these keys have a different behaviour when
you are in Edit mode. Because of this, it is recommended that you use the
Tab key to move from one column to another, as these are guaranteed to
move to the adjacent cell irrespective of whether you are in selection mode
or in Edit mode.

*Use the Tab key to
navigate between
columns in the
datasheet*

Using check boxes

If the value held in a Yes/No field is currently Null, the inside of the check box will be grey.

A field defined using a Yes/No data type will be displayed in a table datasheet using a check box. If the value held in the field is Yes, the check box will display a tick; if the value is No the check box will be empty. Each time you click on a check box Access will set its value to the opposite of what it is currently.

Using the combo box

If a field has been created using the Auto Lookup wizard (or you have set the field's lookup properties yourself), the datasheet will display values from the table to which the field is a Foreign key. These values will be presented using a combo box. When you enter the cell for the particular field, an arrow will appear on the right side of the cell.

To select a value from the combo box, click on the arrow to pull down the list (you can also pull down the list using the keyboard by holding down the Alt key and pressing the down arrow key), and select the required value. If the list is long, you may have to use the scroll bars to the right of the list to display other values.

Cancelling and undoing edits

If you have started to edit a record in a table but have not yet saved the record, you can cancel the changes you have made.

To	Do this
Cancel the changes made to the active cell	Press the Escape key once
Cancel the changes made to the entire record	Press the Escape key twice

If you have already saved the record, you can undo the changes by clicking on the Edit menu and choosing Undo (or by holding down the Control key and pressing the Z key). Access can only undo changes to the last saved record.

Moving and copying data

You can copy and paste entire rows or columns from one table to another provided that the structure of both tables is compatible.

You can use cut, copy and paste in the same way as in other applications. For example, you can cut or copy the contents of one cell and paste it into another cell. Of course, Access will enforce the data type and other integrity constraints defined for the column receiving the pasted data.

Deleting records

To delete a record you must select it first, then delete it. It is much easier to do this using the mouse than it is using the keyboard.

- To select a record using the mouse, click on the grey record selector button to the left of the row in the datasheet.

- To select the record using the keyboard, make sure that the active cell is in the row to be deleted and that the cell is not in Edit mode. Hold down the Shift key and press the space bar.

- To delete the selected record, press the Delete key on the keyboard.

You can select multiple records using the mouse by dragging on the row selector buttons to the left of the rows in the datasheet.

Manipulating data in a table

An Access datasheet provides a number of simple ways to manipulate the data that the table contains. These can be useful if you want to quickly look for values, but they are no match for the powerful data manipulation capabilities provided by a query.

Sorting the rows in a datasheet

You can sort the rows in a table according to the values held in one of its columns. To do this follow these steps.

1. First select the column that holds the values you want to sort by clicking on the column selector button.

2. Now click on the Records menu and choose Sort. When the sub-menu appears choose either Sort Ascending or Sort Descending as appropriate. Alternatively, click on the Sort Ascending or Sort Descending button on the datasheet toolbar.

See Unit 7 for information about the problems that can occur when sorting numbers that have been stored as text.

When you sort in ascending order, Access will put any rows that contain Nulls in the column chosen to sort by at the top of the table. Then it will arrange any rows containing numbers from the smallest value to the largest. Lastly it will show rows containing text values sorted in ascending alphabetical order. If you sort in descending order, this ordering is reversed.

To remove sorting, click on the Records menu and choose Remove filter/sort.

Finding values in a datasheet

Access provides a facility to find values in a datasheet. To find a value in a single column follow these steps.

1. Make sure that the selected cell is in the column in which you want to search. Click on the Edit menu and choose Find (or hold down the Control key and Press the F key). Access will display this dialogue box.

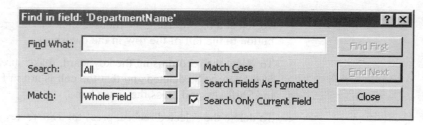

Fig 9.4
The Find dialogue

2. Type the value that you want to find in the Find what: box.

3. To find the first row that contains the value, click on the button labelled Find first. To find the next row (after the current row) that contains the value, click on the button labelled Find next.

The Find dialogue box offers a number of options that increase the power of the search facility. For example, the Match: combo box offers the choice of finding values that are matched by the whole of the field in the datasheet, just the beginning of the field or any part of the field.

Searching in all the fields in a datasheet for a table that contains many records can be extremely slow.

By default Access will only search for values in the currently selected column in the datasheet. If you want to search in all the columns in the datasheet, uncheck the check box labelled Search Only Current Field.

Replacing values in a column

Access also provides a quick and easy way to find and replace values in a table. To do this, follow these steps.

1. Make sure that the selected cell is in the column in which you want to search. Click on the Edit menu and choose Find (or hold down the Control key and Press the # key). Access will display this dialogue box.

Fig 9.5
The Find and
Replace dialogue

2. Make sure that the value that you want to replace is entered correctly in the Find what: box (by default Access will enter the value held in the current cell). Type the value that you want to replace it with in the Replace with: box.

3. To find the next row that contains the value that you want to replace, click on the button labelled Find Next. To verify each value that will be replaced, click on the Replace button.

If you uncheck the check box labelled Match Whole Field, Access will replace the value even if it forms only part of the value in the field. This can be a dangerous thing to do, as the value that you are searching for may form part of a word or part of a field's value that you did not intend to change.

You can replace all matching values by clicking on the button labelled Replace All. Since Access can only undo changes made to the last saved record, this can be a very dangerous thing to do.

Filtering to limit the rows that you see

The Find command helps you to move from one row containing a value to the next row containing the same value. Although this can be useful, it can still be difficult to see the wood for the trees. It is often more helpful to filter the datasheet so that you only see those rows that contain a particular value. Access provides two ways to do this – filtering by selection and filtering by form.

Filter by selection

The simplest way to filter the rows in a table is to select a value in a column, and then instruct Access to show only those records containing that value. This is called filter by selection. To do this, follow these steps.

1. Move the cursor to a cell in the datasheet that holds the value you want to filter by.

2. Click on the Records menu and choose Filter.

3. To show only the rows that contain the value in the current cell, choose Filter by selection from the sub-menu. To show all rows that do not contain the value in the current cell, choose Filter excluding selection from the sub-menu.

To remove filtering, click on the Records menu and choose Remove filter/sort.

When a datasheet has been filtered, Access displays the word Filtered to the right of the datasheet's record navigation buttons.

Filter by form

Filter by selection provides a quick and easy way to filter by a single selected value. To use filter by selection you must first find a row in the datasheet that contains the value. This can be cumbersome. Filter by form provides a more powerful way to filter rows. To use filter by form, follow these steps.

1. Click on the Records menu and choose Filter, then choose Filter by form from the sub-menu. Alternatively, click on the Filter by form button on the toolbar. Access will change the datasheet window so that you no longer see the values in each record. Instead you will see a single blank row. When you move between cells, the current cell will have a down arrow button to the right of the cell. To choose a value to filter by, click on the down arrow and then select a value from the list.

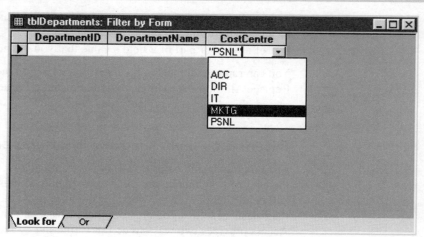

Fig 9.6
Using Filter by form

2. To apply the filter, click on the Records menu and choose Apply filter (or click on the Apply filter button on the toolbar). Access will display the records that meet the criteria entered in the Filter by form selection.

When you click on the Or tab, Access automatically adds another Or tab to the window.

You can choose to filter by more than one value. If you only want to see rows where all the criteria are met, specify the criteria on the first tab of the Filter by form window. If you want to see rows where any of the criteria are met, select the first value to filter by on the first tab of the Filter by form window. Now click on the tab labelled Or at the bottom of the window and select the second value to filter by here.

Using Filter by form you can select values that Access will match exactly or you can specify expressions containing comparison operators. For example, if you wanted to find course offerings before 22 February 1998, you could enter the expression <22/02/1998 in the Filter by form window for the appropriate field in the Course offerings table. For more information about comparison operators, see Appendix A, Using Expressions.

Importing data from another source

These days the automation of an existing manual system is the exception rather than the rule. More often than not a database system is required to replace an existing computerised system. One of the key tasks in the successful implementation of a new system is the accurate conversion of the existing data. However, this is often easier said than done.

What to do with dirty data

The biggest problem when converting and importing data into a new system is the fact that the data that currently exists may not comply with the rules set up for the new system. This may be because of the following factors:

- The integrity constraints set up in the old system do not match those in the new system. Often the old system will not have had any integrity constraints at all. As a result the existing data violates the constraints set up in the new database.

- The old system uses old style or obsolete codes which will need to be converted to the new format.

- The existing data is incomplete.

If the existing data does not meet the integrity constraints set up in the new database, you have to make the choice between relaxing the constraints in the new database to get the data in or spending time cleaning up the data before import. The latter option is obviously the best approach. Unfortunately, in the real world schedule pressure may mean that you do not have the time to spend cleaning up the data, or the decision to choose the first option may be made for you.

If you make the right choice and decide to clean up the data before importing it into the new database, you have to make the decision as to where the data clean up will take place. Here are some of the options.

- **Clean up the data before it is exported from the old system.** This may seem like a good choice because you may be able to get someone else to do it. More often than not, though, it is a non-starter because the people responsible for the old system have too much else to do or may have no commitment to ensuring that the data you get is correct. This is particularly the case if the system you are implementing will replace the current system and their jobs are at risk.

- **Clean up the data as an intermediate process.** This is often a good choice if you can get the data into an intermediate format that can be imported into a spreadsheet such as Microsoft Excel. A spreadsheet provides useful tools for working with data. You can cut and paste ranges, use Find and Replace, create formulas to break up fields into their component parts in separate columns, use AutoFill to copy values down a column, and so on. You can also change the format of numeric or data values into something that will be acceptable to Access.

- **Import the data into a temporary table in the database and clean up the data.** Access provides tools that can be used for updating data in bulk. You can create look up tables to hold conversion values for codes and use update queries to alter values in the temporary table.

Often you will need to use a combination of the last two methods.

Data conversion problems are often underestimated at the beginning of a project. You may have to grapple with issues such as child records that exist without a valid parent record, records that are missing values that are required in the new system, and invalid codes or codes that do not map neatly to new values. You must decide what to do in these cases. Too often the easy option is adopted – get the data in now and let the users of the system sort it all out later. In most cases the sorting out never happens.

Taking on external data

Access provides you with distinct ways of using data from another system. As with other database systems, you can import data from the external source into the table structure defined in your database. In addition, Access provides you with the ability to link the tables used by the other system.

Using linked tables

Access can link tables in a number of formats including tables in another Access database, as well as Paradox, dBase, and FoxPro tables.

If you want to share data with another system you can link tables to your Access database rather than importing the data.

To link a table to an Access database, follow these steps.

1. Click on the File menu and choose Get External Data. From the sub-menu choose Link Tables. The following dialogue will appear.

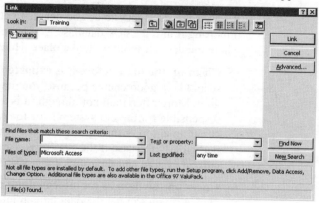

Fig 9.7
Linking to an external data source

2. Select the file that you want to use and click on the Link button. If you are linking to a database that contains multiple tables (such as another Access database), you will see the following dialogue.

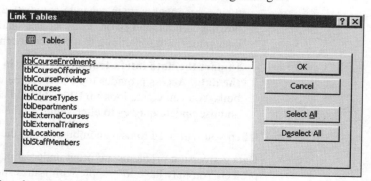

Fig 9.8
The Link Tables dialogue

3. To select a single table, click on its name in the list. You can select multiple tables by holding down the Control key and clicking on each table name in turn. To select a range of names, click on the first table name and then hold down the Shift key and click on the last table name. All tables in between will be selected.

4. When you have completed the selection, click on OK.

Linking tables has the following advantages.

- It avoids the duplication of similar tables in multiple databases. For example, many databases in an organisation hold information about staff members. In our case study we could prevent the possibility of inconsistent data if we could link a Staff member table from the personnel system.

- You can save time and effort in your project if you can use existing data.

As with most things, there are a number of disadvantages to using linked tables.

- Your system may know nothing of the way that business rules are enforced in other applications that use the tables concerned. Your system could unwittingly enter invalid data into the table.

- You will have no control over the integrity constraints in the other database.

- Clear rules need to be set up regarding the responsibility for updating the data. Like all shared resources, the state of the data in a shared table will quickly degrade if no one 'owns' the data and is responsible for its quality.

In practice it is best only to read data from linked tables and not to write data to these tables. If data needs to be updated in linked tables, it is best done through the application that 'owns' the tables where integrity constraints are defined and enforced.

Do note that if you have decided to split your database into two separate files (as described in Unit 6), linking is the means by which you attach the tables at the back end to the front end database that contains the forms, queries and reports.

Importing external data

If you are converting from an existing system that will be retired when the new system becomes available, you will want to do a one-off import of the data. Access has been designed to be able to import data from most other popular PC formats.

Even if Access does not support the current format directly, it is usually possible to export from the current system in a format that Access will be able to import. On occasions you may have to resort to the lowest common denominator by using text files.

Access provides wizards that simplify the process of importing files in most formats.

Access also provides a Table analyser wizard that is designed to assist you in the process of normalising your data. While this is a nice idea, it is better to understand how to do this yourself for the following reasons:

- The wizard makes choices based on a set of arbitrary rules, not on an understanding of the data. For this reason the wizard is often unable to offer any suggestions to assist in normalising the data.

- Even if the wizard does successfully split your data into several tables, you may not understand why. As a result you may not be able to correctly make changes to the data model if you need to store additional data items. In addition, you may not be able to create queries that will recreate the original view of the data.

Revision exercises

1. Is it important to have established all the constraints in a database before entering data? Give reasons for your answer.

2. Describe the ways in which an Access datasheet differs from a spreadsheet in terms of the way that data is saved.

3. What factors can make datasheets difficult to use?

4. What are the main problems that could occur when data has to be converted from one system for use in another system?

10 Using forms

What you will learn in this unit

This unit describes how to use forms to capture new data and edit existing data in a database. At the end of this unit you should:

- ❏ be able to create a new form using the wizards provided with Access
- ❏ be able to view and edit data using a form
- ❏ be able to customise a form created by the wizard
- ❏ understand how forms can be used to view and edit data from multiple tables.

Why use a form?

Datasheets provide a limited view of your data. Some types of data such as Object Linking and Embedding (OLE) objects cannot be viewed at all using a datasheet. Forms provide you with the means to present your data how you want. With a form you can:

- present your data in a similar manner to a paper-based form
- present your data in an appealing way using graphical devices such a lines, shading and colours
- control the order in which data is entered into fields
- do calculations on the data in the form
- show data from more than one table
- show meaningful descriptions of values rather than codes
- automate common tasks.

Access provides a number of tools that simplify the process of creating forms.

AutoForm

To create a form quickly, use AutoForm. AutoForm creates a form that shows all the fields in a table (or query) in the order that they would appear in datasheet view. To create a form based on a table using AutoForm follow these steps.

Important: At this stage the form design has not been saved.

1. Click on the table tab in the database window. Now click on the name of the table whose data you want to display in the form.

2. Click on the AutoForm button on the toolbar. Access will create a new form containing all the fields in the selected table.

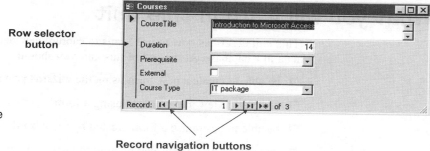

Row selector button

Record navigation buttons

Fig 10.1
A form created by the Access AutoForm wizard

To save the form design, click on the File menu then choose Save Form As. In the Save dialogue box, enter a name for the form and choose OK.

A form created by AutoForm displays one record at a time. Each field is arranged in a column down the length of the form.

Creating a form using a wizard

AutoForm will always create a form that shows a single record in a vertical column, with the same sort of appearance. If you want more control over the type of form that is created or how the form appears, you can use a wizard.

The wizard takes you through a series of steps that allow you to select the fields that you want to appear on the form and to choose from a predefined selection of formats.

Even if you do not particularly like the format provided by the wizard, using the wizard can save a lot of time and effort. If you don't like the final result, you can always adjust the design of the form after the wizard has finished.

Working with forms

When you create a form based on a table using the wizard, it creates a link between the form and the table. The technical term is that the form is 'bound' to the table. When you enter data into the database using a form, the data is still stored in the table – the form provides a window into the data, but the table is still used to store the data.

See Unit 8 for information about defining a lookup in a table.

The data in the table to which the form is bound is displayed in controls on the form. There are various types of controls – the most common type of control is a text box, which can be used to show both numbers and text. The wizards may also create other types of control on the form. If a field has a Yes/No data type, the wizard will create a check box on the form. If a lookup has been defined on a field in the table design, the wizard will use the type of control specified in the Display control property of the table design.

Viewing and editing data using a form

Most of the techniques that you use for viewing and editing data using a datasheet apply to a form. You use the Tab key to move from one control to the next and Shift + Tab to move back through the controls. If you press the Tab key when you are in the last control on the form, the form will display the next record. You can navigate through the records using the record navigation buttons in the same way as for a datasheet window. The form also has a row selector button to enable you to select the record.

Changing the form design

You can also view a datasheet that shows the records to which a form is bound.

In the same way that there are two views of a table (Design View and Datasheet View) there are also several views of a form. When you use the form to display the data from a table, you are in Form View. If you want to change the design of a form, you must open it in Design View. In Design View the form does not show any values from the table to which it is bound.

To open a form in Design View, select the form in the database window then click on the button labelled Design. You can switch between the three views of a form that is already open by clicking on the View menu and choosing one of the first three options (Design View, Form View, Datasheet View), or by clicking on the View button on the toolbar. The following figure shows a form open in Design View.

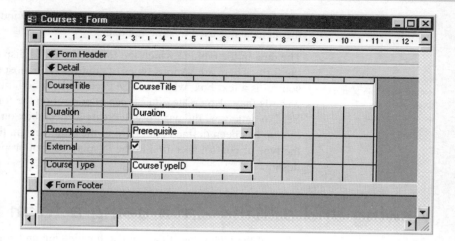

Fig 10.2
The form in Design
View

Parts of the form

The form is divided in to three sections as follows.

- **Header** – anything in this section of the form will always appear at the top of the form. As you navigate through the records using the form, the values displayed in the form header will remain constant.

- **Details** – this section appears between the header and the footer. As you navigate through the records the data in this section will change according to display the data in the underlying record.

- **Footer** – anything in this section of the form will always appear at the bottom of the form. As you navigate through the records using the form, the values displayed in the form footer will remain constant.

Selecting, re-sizing and moving controls

When you work with a form in Design View you can change the location, size and arrangement of the controls on the form. To change the appearance or position of a control, you must click on it to select it. When the control is selected it will appear as follows.

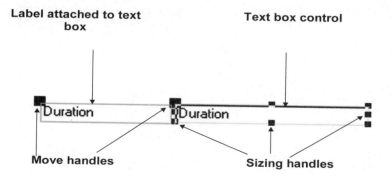

Fig 10.3
Moving and sizing a
control on a form

Now that the control is selected, you can move and size it as follows.

To	Do this
Move the control to a new position	Click on the control. Move the mouse pointer until it appears as a hand with all its fingers outstretched. Now drag to move the control to its new position.
Move the control to a new position independently of its attached label	Click on the control, position the mouse pointer over the move handle until the shape of the mouse pointer changes to a hand with a single finger pointing. Now drag the control to its new position.
Make the control taller or shorter	Drag on the size handle in the middle of one of the horizontal edges of the control.
Make the control wider or narrower	Drag on the size handle in the middle of one of the vertical edges of the control.
Do both	Drag on the size handle on the corner of the control.

Selecting multiple controls

If you want to simultaneously move or size multiple controls there are various techniques to select more than one control.

1. Drag on an empty part of the form (that is, somewhere on the form that does not contain any controls). You will see the outline of a rectangle start to appear. Keep dragging until some part of the controls that you want to select are within this rectangle. Let go of the mouse button – all the controls that were anywhere within the rectangle will be selected. This technique is called 'rubber banding'. You can also use this technique by dragging in the rulers to the top and the side of the form in Design View.

2. Click on the first control that you want to select. Now press the shift key and click on the next control that you want to select. Both controls will now be selected. Continue until you have selected all the required controls.

Changing the appearance of a control

The formatting toolbar provides a number of methods for changing the format of a control on a form. The formatting applies to the selected control or group of controls. The following figure shows each item on the formatting toolbar.

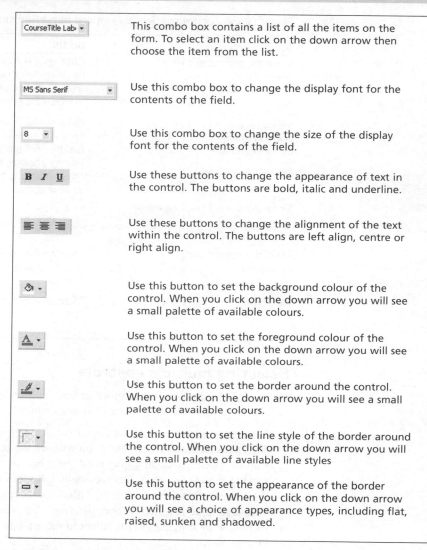

Fig 10.4
Items on the
formatting toolbar

The combo box and toolbar descriptions shown in the figure:

This combo box contains a list of all the items on the form. To select an item click on the down arrow then choose the item from the list.

Use this combo box to change the display font for the contents of the field.

Use this combo box to change the size of the display font for the contents of the field.

Use these buttons to change the appearance of text in the control. The buttons are bold, italic and underline.

Use these buttons to change the alignment of the text within the control. The buttons are left align, centre or right align.

Use this button to set the background colour of the control. When you click on the down arrow you will see a small palette of available colours.

Use this button to set the foreground colour of the control. When you click on the down arrow you will see a small palette of available colours.

Use this button to set the border around the control. When you click on the down arrow you will see a small palette of available colours.

Use this button to set the line style of the border around the control. When you click on the down arrow you will see a small palette of available line styles

Use this button to set the appearance of the border around the control. When you click on the down arrow you will see a choice of appearance types, including flat, raised, sunken and shadowed.

Adding fields to the form

Unfortunately you cannot use the wizards to make changes to existing forms.

When you create a form using the wizard, you can select the fields that you want to display on the form. However, after the wizard has finished creating the form you may change your mind and want to add fields to the form. In Design View you can add fields to a bound form in one of two ways.

Using the field list

When a form is bound to a table or a query you can use the Field list to display a list of the fields that appear in the bound table or query. To show the Field list, click on the View menu and choose Field list. Alternatively, click on the Field list button on the Form design toolbar.

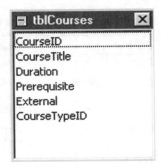

Fig 10.5
The Field list

To add a field to the form, click on the name of the field in the Field list, then drag it onto the form.

Using the toolbox

The toolbox is a special toolbar that contains a button for each of the different types of control that you can create on a form. To show the toolbox, click on the View menu and choose Toolbox. Alternatively, click on the Toolbox button on the Form design toolbar. Figure 10.6 shows each of the buttons on the toolbox.

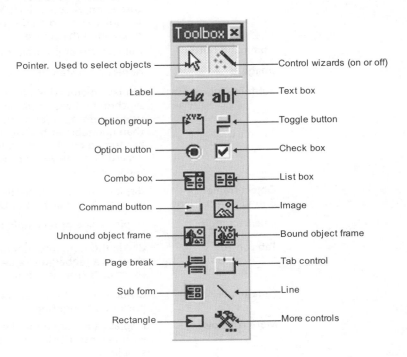

Fig 10.6
The tool box

Types of controls

Each type of control can be used for a particular purpose.

Control type	Used to
Pointer	keep one tool active until you select another one
Control wizard	if this button is pressed, a wizard is invoked to help you when you create a new control on the form or report
Label	display descriptive text such as a title, a caption, or instructions on a form or report
Text box	display data consisting of text, numbers and symbols
Option group	display a group frame to which you add check boxes, option buttons or toggle buttons that represent numerical data values. If control wizards are turned on, Access will launch the option group wizard to guide you through the process of creating the control.
Toggle button Option button Check box	display Yes/No values. Can be used to show the individual items in an option group.
Combo box List box	display a list of values to choose from. Can show values from another table or values that are stored in the control. If control wizards are turned on, Access will launch the combo box or list box wizard to guide you through the process of creating the control.
Command button	call a macro or program to automate processing
Image	display a constant picture
Subform/Subreport	display an embedded form or report which can be synchronised with data on the current form. By using subforms a form can display data from more than one table at the same time. If control wizards are turned on, Access will launch the sub form wizard to guide you through the process of creating the control.
Object frame Bound object frame	display a picture, embedded document or spreadsheet or any other OLE object
Line/Rectangle	display a line or rectangle on the form or report
Tab control	divide the form into separate tabbed pages like those in a tabbed dialogue. Can be useful for saving space on a crowded form.
Page break	divide the form into separate pages for display purposes, or printing
More controls	Displays a dialogue that lists other controls supplied with Microsoft Office, or bought from other suppliers.

Creating a bound control using the toolbox

To create a control that is bound to a field in the underlying table or query, follow these steps.

1. Click on the button for the required type of control in the toolbox.

2. Click on the name of the control in the Field list and drag it into the required position on the form.

3. If the control wizards are turned on, the wizard for that particular type of control will start. Follow the steps in the wizard to complete the creation of the control.

Creating an unbound control using the toolbox

For more information about expressions, see Appendix A.

To create an unbound control on a form, first click on the button for the required type of control in the toolbox. Now drag on the surface of the form to create a control of the required size. You can use an unbound control to show calculated values on a form. To do this you must set the control's Control source property to a valid expression to perform the calculation.

Deleting a control

If you no longer require a control on a form you can delete it. To delete a control, follow these steps.

1. Click on the control to select it.

2. Press the Delete key on the keyboard (or click on the Edit menu and choose Delete).

Further enhancing the form design

The design tools discussed so far can be used to produce professional looking forms that will assist in the capture and display of data in the database. Once you have become familiar with the use of these tools you may wish to be able to customise your forms even more. Access provides you with almost total control over the appearance and behaviour of forms.

Using the properties sheet

Many of the design tools described above automate the process of setting properties for the individual elements of the form. Each element (the form itself, each section on the form and each control on the form) has its own set of properties. These properties control the appearance or behaviour of the element. To display the properties sheet, do the following.

1. Select the item for which you want to see the Properties.

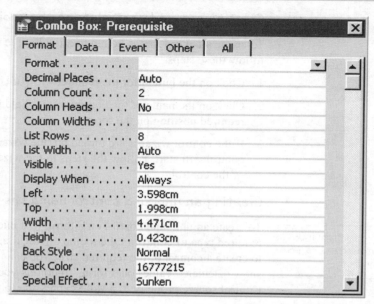

Fig 10.7
The Properties
window

2. Click on the View menu and choose Properties. You can also click on the
    Properties button on the Form design toolbar, or simply double click on
    the object. You will see the Properties window.

To find out what a
property does, click on
the name of the
property in the
Properties window, then
press the F1 key on the
keyboard. Access will
display the Help topic
associated with the
property.

The Properties window is a tabbed dialogue box. Properties are organised
according to their purpose. For example, all the properties that control the
appearance of an object can be found on the Format tab. To see all the
properties for an object, click on the All tab.

Please note, before you change any properties you should take care to ensure
that you are working with the properties for the correct object. If you click
on another object on the form, the Properties window will show the
properties for that object. The title bar of the Properties window shows the
type of object that is selected together with its name.

Some properties hold values that can be changed by typing in a new value
into the box in the Properties window. For example, the Top property for a
control expects a number representing the distance from its top border to the
top edge of the section in which it is contained. The distance is defined in
the units of measurement indicated (inches or centimetres).

Other properties present a list of values from which you can select. For
example, the decimal places property for a control will display a list of
integer values, or Auto. Some properties will display a button with an
ellipsis (three dots) on it when selected. When you click on this button,
Access will launch a wizard or builder to help to select the appropriate
value.

You can change almost all the attributes of a form using its properties. For
example, you can choose whether to display the navigation buttons at the
bottom of the form or whether the row selector button is visible. You can

even control the appearance of the window that holds the form by changing its border style, or choose whether to display the window's maximise or minimise buttons or the control box in the top corner.

Setting the tab order

When you create a form using the wizard, the controls on the form are arranged in the same order that they appear in the table design. This means that if you use the tab key to move between the controls on the form, the cursor moves in this sequence. As you add or delete controls to the form, this order will change and the tab key will not move between controls in the order that they appear on the form. To change the tab order for a form, follow these steps.

1. Click on the View menu and choose Tab Order. The Tab Order dialogue box will be displayed.

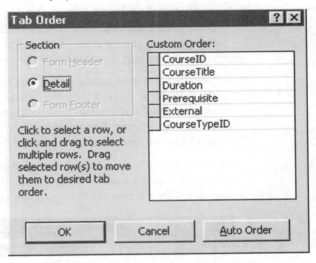

Fig 10.8
Changing the tab order

2. To change the tab order, click on the row selector button next to the name of the control that you want to move.

3. Now drag the row selector button up or down. You will see a line moving on the lines between the control names. This line indicates the position in the tab order in which the control will be placed. When the line is in the correct place, let go of the mouse button to drop the control name.

Changing the tab order does not physically move the controls on the form. You can set the tab order so that it matches the physical arrangement of the controls on the form by clicking on the button labelled Auto Order.

Creating a form that shows records from multiple tables

A common requirement in database applications is to show records from more than one table at the same time. In most cases the requirement is to show data from two tables that have a one-to-many relationship. For example, in an order processing system you may want a form that shows details of the order at the top of the form and each line item for that order in the bottom of the form. Access provides the means to do this using a main form and sub form combination. To create a main form/sub form combination follow these steps.

1. First create the main form (you can use AutoForm or one of the wizards to do this). The main form is based on the table on the one side of the relationship.

2. Now open the main form in Design View. Click on the Sub form control button in the toolbox, then drag on the form to draw an outline of where the control will be placed. The Sub form control wizard will start and take you through the steps needed to create the sub form.

3. Provided you have established a relationship between the tables on which the main form and sub form are based, Access will know how to synchronise the records in the two forms. If it does not, you may have to specify the Primary key and Foreign key fields in the LinkMasterFields and LinkChildFields properties of the Sub form control.

An example of a main form/sub form combination is shown below. The main form shows a Courses Offerings table. The sub form shows all the enrolments for the course offering shown in the main form.

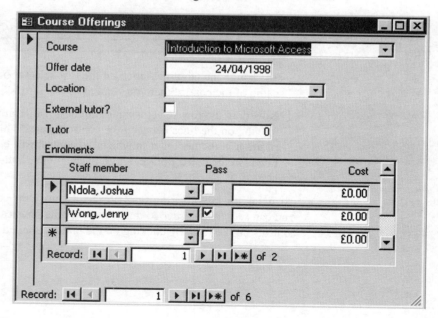

Fig 10.9
Showing data from two tables using a main form and sub form

As you move through the records in the main form, Access will synchronise the sub form so that it shows only the related records.

One of the most powerful capabilities in a fully normalised data model implemented in a relational database is the ability to view the data from many different points of view. The form above shows all the enrolments for a particular course offering. In a data entry situation, this form could be used to allocate enrolments to a particular course.

The form below shows all the courses that a particular staff member has attended. The data that this form shows is essentially the same as that shown in the form above, and if the data is changed in either of these forms, it will be reflected in the other form.

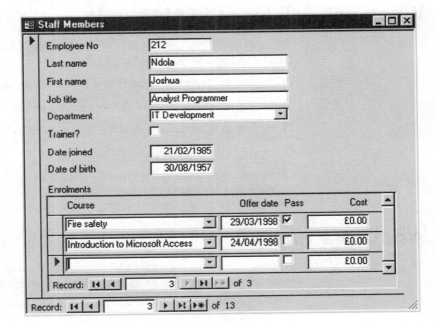

Fig 10.10
Data from the same two tables viewed through another main form/sub form combination

Revision exercises

1. What are the main benefits of using forms instead of datasheets?

2. Describe the ways that you add new controls to a form that is bound to a table or query?

3. How can you get help regarding a property of a control on a form?

4. What is the significance of the tab order?

11 Using queries

What you will learn in this unit

This unit describes how to use queries to process the data in a database. At the end of this unit you should:

❐ be able to create a new query and choose the fields that you require

❐ be able to specify a sort order for the data selected by the query

❐ be able to filter the data selected by the query using criteria

❐ be able to create calculated fields in a query

❐ be able to create a query based on more than one table and change how the tables are joined together.

What is a query?

A query is the most important tool for turning the data in a database into information. A query can be used to ask questions about your data. With a query you can:

• choose which fields you want to see

• choose which records you want to see (filter the data)

• change the order in which the records appear (sort the data)

• see data from more than one table at the same time

• derive new values from the existing values in a table

• perform calculations on the data

• make automatic changes to data in the underlying tables.

The most common type of query is called a 'select query'. When you run a select query from the database window it displays the results of the query in a datasheet. In most cases you can edit the data that appears in the datasheet in the same way that you can edit data in a datasheet view of a table.

Where can you use queries?

As you will see in Unit 14, most reports are based on queries.

Access uses queries in many places. If you save a query in the database, you can run it from the database window. You can also base forms and reports on stored queries.

You will also find that settings for some property values may be queries. For example, the Row Source property of a list box or combo box can be set to a stored query, or you can build a query using the query builder. In addition, when you create an advanced filter for a datasheet or form, you are actually creating a query.

Creating a new query

To create a new query, select the Queries tab in the database window and then click on the New button. You can use the wizards provided with Access to create many different queries, or you can design the query from scratch.

To design the query without the help of the wizard, select Design View from the list of options in the New query dialogue box. Access will prompt you to specify the table or tables from which the query will retrieve data.

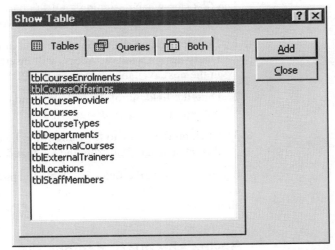

Fig 11.1
The Show Table dialogue box enables you to choose the tables to include in the query

A query can be based on a table or on another query. The Show Table dialogue box lists tables and queries separately on different tabs and together on the tab called Both. To add a table to the query, select the table in the list then click on the Add button. When you have finished adding tables to the query, click on the Close button.

You complete the design of the query in the Query design window shown in Fig 11.2.

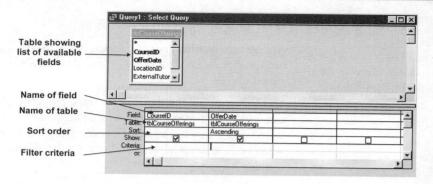

Table showing list of available fields

Name of field

Name of table

Sort order

Filter criteria

Fig 11.2
The Query design window

The Query design window uses a format based on Query By Example (QBE), which was originally developed by IBM in the 1970s. For this reason, the grid is often referred to as the QBE grid.

The Query design window is divided into two panes. The top pane shows the tables that have been added to the query. This pane looks and behaves like the relationship window. Each table appears in its own box that contains a list of the fields in the table. The bottom pane of the window is arranged as a grid. Each column in the grid can hold a field from a table that provides data for the query.

Choosing the fields you want in your query

The first step when designing a select query is to specify which fields you want to see in the query result. To do this you have three choices.

1. Double click on the name of the field in the table box at the top of the Query design window. Access will insert the field's name in the field row in the next available column in the QBE grid.

2. Drag the field out of the table box and drop it onto the QBE grid at the bottom of the Query design window.

3. Click on the arrow to the right of the Field name box in the QBE grid, then choose the field from the list that drops down.

If you want all of the fields in a table to appear in the query results you can choose the * in the table box. This provides a quick and easy way to show all the fields in the table in the results of the query.

Saving the query design

Like other Access objects, the design of a query is not stored in the database until you explicitly save it. To save the query design, carry out these steps.

1. Click on the File menu and choose Save (or click on the Save button on the query design toolbar).

2. Type the name that you want to give to the query in the box labelled Query name, then choose OK.

By default Access will call the first query that you create Query1, the second Query2 and so on. As your database grows, you will create more and more queries and these meaningless names will not help you if you need to change a particular query. You should give each query a meaningful name that describes its purpose.

Running the query

To see the results of the query you must run the query. To do this click on the Query menu and choose Run, or click on the Run button on the query design toolbar. When you run a query that selects data from the database, the Query design window changes to a datasheet.

Specifying a sort order

To specify a sort order for the rows returned by the query, click on the arrow to the right of the Sort box in the QBE grid for the column you want to sort by. Access will offer the choice of sorting in ascending or descending order. If you want to stop sorting on a particular column, choose Not sorted from this list.

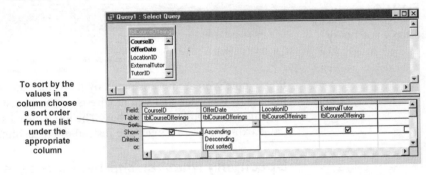

To sort by the values in a column choose a sort order from the list under the appropriate column

Fig 11.3
Choosing the sort order for a field.

You can specify a sort order for more than one field in a query. If a query contains more than one field with a sort order, Access will sort from left to right. This means that Access will sort the rows according to the values held in the left most column with a sort order. If any rows have identical values in this column, Access will sort these rows according to the values in the next column to the right with a sort order specified.

Top value queries

Access also provides the ability to limit the rows returned by a sorted query to the top most sub-set of values. For example, you may want to see only the five most expensive courses. To do this, follow these steps.

1. Create the query and add the required fields to the query grid.

2. Choose the sort order required for the appropriate field. For example, to see the five most expensive courses you would sort by Cost in descending order; to see the five least expensive courses you would sort by Cost in ascending order.

3. Click on the Top values list box on the Query design toolbar and choose the number of top or bottom values that you want to see.

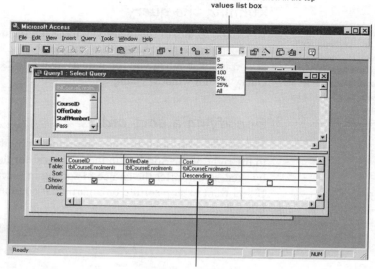

Choose the number of values to show in the top values list box

Choose descending sort order to see the five most expensive courses

Fig 11.4
Selecting options for
a top value query

Please note, you are not restricted by the values that appear in the top values list box. If the value that you require is not in the list, you can simply type the value that you want in the box. The top values list box will also accept a value expressed as a percentage instead of an absolute number.

Specifying whether the field appears in the query result

There may be times when you want to sort on a field but do not want the values held in that field to appear in the Query result datasheet. For example, you may want to sort a list of employees by grade or salary, but not want to show the grade or salary amount in the query's output. To specify that a field should not appear in the query results, uncheck the check box in the Show row for the appropriate column in the QBE grid. If this box is ticked this column will appear in the query's output, if it is empty the column will not appear.

Renaming a field in the query

You can specify a different name for any column that appears in the results of a query For example, you may want the EmployeeNo column from the Staff members table to appear as Staff number. You can do this in one of two ways. Either:

a. click on the name of the column that you want to rename in the QBE grid

b. display the query properties window by clicking on the View menu and choosing Properties (or click on the Properties button on the Query design toolbar)

c. type the name that you want to appear in the column heading in the Caption property.

Or:

a. click in front of the name of the column that you want to rename in the QBE grid

b. type the name that you want to appear in the column heading followed by a colon in front of the field name in the table.

Type the new name, followed by a colon, in front of the field name

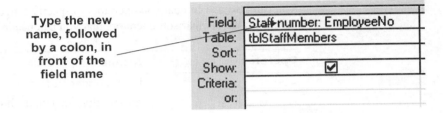

Fig 11.5
Renaming a field

Choosing the rows that you see by specifying criteria

One of the most important reasons for using a query is to filter the rows so that you see only the rows that are of interest to you. For example, you may only be interested in the data for staff members in a particular department, or in course offerings for a particular course. To filter the rows that are returned by the query, you specify criteria for a column against which the values in the column are compared.

Specifying criteria to filter the results of the query

If you type a text value in the Criteria row, Access will automatically put double quotes around it.

You specify criteria in the Criteria row of the QBE grid. If you want to see only those rows where a column holds a particular value, you simply type the value that you want to find in the Criteria row under the appropriate column.

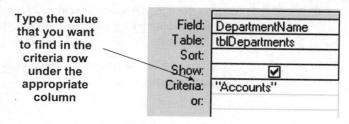

Fig 11.6
Specifying criteria for a field

Type the value that you want to find in the criteria row under the appropriate column

If you enter a value like this, the query will show only those records that match the value exactly. Access compares the value in each row of the table against the value you have entered. Only those rows that match the criteria will appear in the resulting datasheet.

You can also use comparison operators to specify ranges of values to find. These are the comparison operators that you can use in an Access query.

Operator	Means
<	less than specified value
>	greater than specified value
<>	not equal to specified value
<=	less than or equal to specified value
>=	greater than or equal to specified value
Between ... And ...	between two specified values

For example, to show only those courses that last less than seven hours you would specify the criteria <7 in the criteria row under the Duration column of the Courses table.

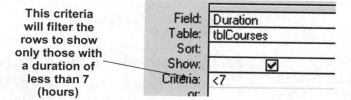

Fig 11.7
Specifying criteria using a comparison operator

This criteria will filter the rows to show only those with a duration of less than 7 (hours)

Please note, if you type a date value under a date column, Access will automatically place # symbols around the dates. For example, if you typed

Between 01/01/1998 And 01/03/1998

in the criteria row under the OfferDate column for the Course offerings table, Access will automatically change this to:

Between #01/01/1998# And #01/03/1998#

Text comparisons using wild cards

You can also provide criteria that instruct Access to find partial matches in text fields. To do this you use two special 'wild card' characters. When you use a wild card character, Access automatically will put the word 'Like' in front of what you have typed. Like is a special operator that is used to indicate a wild card comparison.

You can use the following wild card characters with the Like operator.

Wild card character	Does
?	Matches any value that has any single character in the same position as the question mark. For example, Like "Sm?th" will return both Smith and Smyth, but not Smithers.
*	Matches any number of characters in the same position as asterisk. For example, Like "*guay" would find Paraguay and Uruguay. Like "*fire*" would return the rows that had the word 'fire' anywhere at all in the field.

Selections based on more than one value

Access allows you to specify multiple values as criteria for a query. You do this when you want to see the rows in a table that match one value, plus all the rows that match another value. Access provides a number of different ways to do this. One way is to type the two values on different rows under the same column in the QBE grid. Another way is to type the first value in the QBE grid, followed by the word Or and then the second value.

Fig 11.8
Two ways to specify more than one comparison value in the criteria

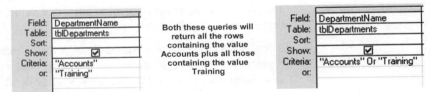

These techniques will work just as well when searching for more than two values. However, Access provides an easier way to find the rows that match a list of criteria. This is the 'In' operator. When you use In, the list of values for comparison must be enclosed in brackets and separated by commas. For example, to see only those rows for the accounts, personnel and training departments, you would type this in the criteria row under the Department name column:

In ("Accounts","Personnel","Training")

Selecting rows by excluding values

You can also filter records by excluding certain values. With simple values you can use the 'not equal to' operator. For example, to exclude all rows with a value of 5 in a column you would type the following in the criteria row:

<>5

This will return all rows except those that have 5 in the specified column. When using wild card searches using Like, or specifying value lists using In, you must use the 'Not' operator to exclude the values that you do not want. For example, to find all rows that do not contain the ending 'guay', you would type the following in the criteria row of the QBE grid:

Not Like "*guay"

To exclude a list of values, you would type:

Not In ("Accounts","Personnel","Training")

This would return all the rows except those for the accounts, personnel and training departments.

The problem with Null values

See Unit 7 for more information about Nulls.

Imagine you have a table that contains 50 rows. The table has a numeric column that can contain integer values. You specify a criteria of 50 in the criteria row for this column in a query. The query returns 20 rows. Now you change the criteria to <>50. How many rows would you expect the query to return? If the column contains any Null values, the answer will not be 30 rows. The problem is the fact that a Null represents an unknown or missing value. A Null value is never equal to any other value, nor is it unequal to any other value.

To cope with the fact that a Null will never match explicit criteria, Access provides two special expressions for matching Null values. To find any rows that contain Null in a column, you must specify the following expression in the criteria row of the QBE grid for that column.

Is Null

To find any rows that do not contain Null in a column, you must specify the following expression.

Is Not Null

Specifying criteria for more than one column

So far we have looked at queries that specify criteria for a single column. You can also create queries that specify criteria on more than one column.

However, how the query behaves depends on where you type the criteria in the QBE grid.

If you only want to see the rows that contain values that match both of the criteria, you must type the criteria on the same Criteria row in the QBE grid.

Fig 11.9
This query will only return rows that match both criteria specified

Criteria on the
same row in
the QBE grid

For example, to see the course offerings that fall between 1/1/1997 and 1/3/1997 and are taught by an external trainer, you would need to specify the criteria as in Figure 11.9.

If you only want to see the rows that contain values that match either of the criteria, you must type the criteria on different criteria rows in the QBE grid.

Fig 11.10
This query will return rows that match either of the criteria specified

Criteria on
different rows
in the QBE
grid

For example, to see the course offerings that fall between 1/1/1997 and 1/3/1997 or those are taught by an external trainer, you would specify the criteria as in Figure 11.10.

Mixing up And and Or conditions is one of the most frequent causes of incorrect results being returned by a query.

You will often see the first type of query referred to as using And conditions and the second as using Or conditions. A query that uses And conditions is much more restrictive that one that uses Or conditions. As a result, the second query will return many more rows than the first.

Creating calculated columns

For more information about expressions, see Appendix A.

A calculated column uses data in the tables on which the query is based but performs a calculation on the data to return a new value that is not stored in the table. To create a calculated field, you must specify an expression that tells Access how to perform the calculation. You can enter any valid expression to produce a calculated field.

For example, you may want to calculate the extended price for an item in an ordering system. To create the calculated field, type a name for the field in the Field name box in the QBE grid, followed by a colon, and then followed by the expression that performs the calculation. For example:

    Extension : QtyOrdered * UnitPrice

When this query is run the datasheet will contain a column headed Extension. This column will contain the result of multiplying the value held in the QtyOrdered field by the UnitPrice field in each row.

You can also join the contents of two text fields together using the text concatenation operator (&). For example, to join an employee's surname and first name together, you could enter this in the field name:

FullName : LastName & ", " & FirstName

You can also use many of the built-in functions that are supplied with Access, some of which are described in Appendix A.

Queries based on more than one table

Queries in Access can be based on more than one table. To add another table to a query, display the 'Show table' dialogue box by clicking on the Query menu and choosing Show table (or click on the Show table button on the query design toolbar). Select the required table or tables in the list and then click on the Add button. When you have finished adding tables to the query, click on the Close button.

The lines between tables show how they will be joined in the query

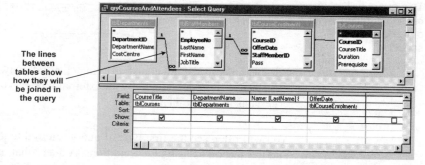

Fig 11.11
A query can retrieve data from more than one table

If there is a relationship defined between the tables in the query, Access will show the join line between the tables in the Query design window based on the relationship that has been defined. If no relationship has been defined, Access will join the tables that share the same name (if any).

If you do not specify a join between two tables in a query, Access will simply join every row in the first table to every row in the second table.

If Access does not correctly work out how the tables are joined together, you can specify a join by dragging the joining field in one table onto the joining field in the other table (in the same way as in the Relationships window).

When you join two tables together in a query, Access will join all the rows in the first table with all the rows in the second table that have a matching value in the column on which they are joined. For example, joining the Staff members table to the Departments table gives the result in Figure 11.12.

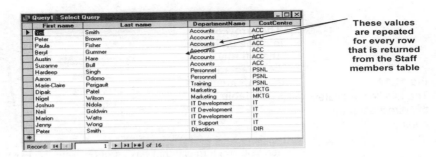

These values are repeated for every row that is returned from the Staff members table

Fig 11.12
The results of a query based on more than one table in Datasheet View

Notice that, although the department name and cost centre occur only once in the Departments table, Access repeats these values for each row that is returned from the Staff members table.

In technical terms, this is called an 'equi-join.'

However, what if a member of staff has not been assigned to a department? This query only returns rows where there is a matching value in both of the columns on which the join is made. If the join column in either table contains a Null value, that row will be excluded from the results of the query. Because of this any unassigned employees will be omitted from the results of the query. If you want to see every member of staff, even if they are currently unassigned, you need to alter the join between the two tables.

Changing the join property

To change the join property, first click on the join line between the tables in the Query design window. The join line should appear darker to show that it is selected. Now double-click on the join line. The Join Properties dialogue box shown below will be displayed.

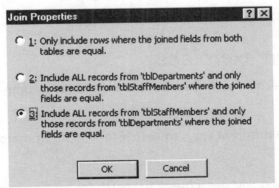

Fig 11.13
The Join Properties window

This type of query that preserves all the rows from one of the tables is called an 'outer-join' query.

The dialogue box allows you to specify from which table you want to return all the rows. Because we want to see all the rows in the Staff members table, the third option has been chosen. When you click on the OK button and return to the Query design window you will see that the join line in the Query design window has changed to show an arrow pointing away from the table from which all records will be retrieved.

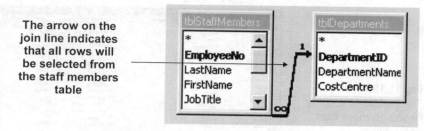

The arrow on the join line indicates that all rows will be selected from the staff members table

Fig 11.14
The join line indicates the direction of the outer-join

When you run a query that has an outer-join, Access will return all the rows from the preserved table, even if there is no matching row in the other table.

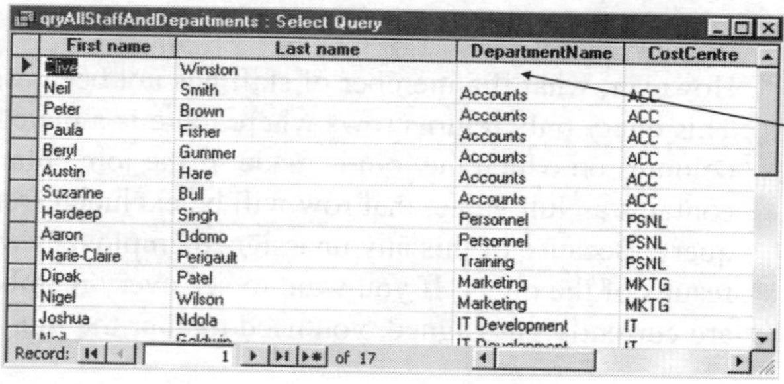

Fig 11.15
A query with an outer-join can return Null values, even if the tables concerned do not contain any Nulls

This staff member is currently unassigned. The query returns Nulls where there is no matching value

The columns that would normally show a value from the other table will contain Null values.

Revision exercises

1. If you specify a sort order on more than one column in a query, how will Access sort the data?

2. Give two different ways to search for rows that match any one of three values in a single field.

3. How would you use a query to search for missing values in a table?

4. How can a query return Nulls even if these are no Nulls in the tables on which the query is based?

12 Totals queries

What you will learn in this unit

This unit describes how to use queries that group and aggregate data. These queries can be used to summarise data and calculate descriptive statistics based on the data values. At the end of this unit you should:

❏ understand why totals queries are useful for producing information from a database

❏ be able to create a totals query that summarises data

❏ understand the purpose and behaviour of each of the aggregate functions that are available in totals queries

❏ understand the different ways to filter data by using criteria in a totals query.

Why use a totals query?

Management often requires summarised information regarding the operations of an organisation. These requests may take the form of a question such as how many staff members have attended the staff induction course so far this year, or what is the total number of staff in each department? In traditional information systems a great deal of programmer effort was expended developing reports that answered these types of questions. Microsoft Access provides a type of query called a totals query that simplifies the task of answering questions such as these.

Grouping and summarising data is the foundation of most management reports.

Totals queries allow you to partition your data into groups and to calculate summary information for each group. The values in the table or tables determine the groupings. Each group in a totals query is mutually exclusive.

To create a totals query, follow these steps.

1. Create a new query as described in Unit 11. Add the fields that you need to include in the query to the query grid.

2. Now click on the View menu and choose Totals (or click on the Totals button on the Query design toolbar). An additional row will appear on the query grid with the word Total to the left. To begin with each column in the query will have the words "Group By" in this row.

3. If you want to group by the values in a particular column, leave the words "Group By" in the Total row. If you want to summarise the data, you need to change this value from "Group By" to a summary function in each column that you want to summarise. To do this click in the Total row under the appropriate column. Now click on the button with the down arrow and select the summary function you require (these functions are described in detail below).

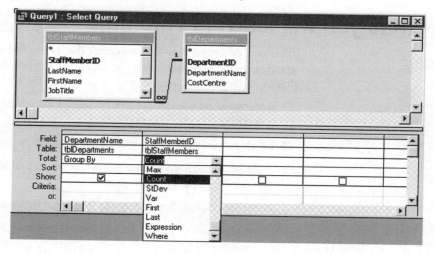

Fig 12.1
Choosing a summary function in a totals query. This query will tell you how many staff are in each department

4. When you have chosen a summary function for each column you want to summarise, run the query in the normal way. The results of a totals query are displayed in a datasheet like other queries. You will see one row for each data value in the last "Group By" column.

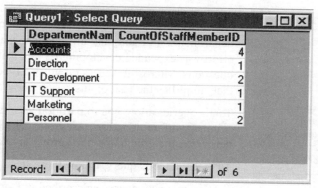

Fig 12.2
The results of the totals query in a datasheet window

The column heading for the summarised columns will reflect the calculation that is being performed. As you can see in Figure 12.2, a count of a column named StaffMemberID will result in a column called CountOfStaffMemberID.

Please note, totals queries cannot be updated. Each row in a totals query displays data that is derived from several rows in the underlying table. Because the rows returned by a totals query do not relate to individual rows in the table on which they are based, Access is unable to determine which row or rows to update.

Grouping data

Analysing data in this way is often referred to as 'slicing and dicing'.

When you apply grouping to the values in a particular column, you are partitioning the complete set of values in that column into sub-sets. Each sub-set is separate to each other sub-set (there are no overlaps) and you can reassemble the original set by combining all the sub-sets. You can picture this as being like the slices in a sliced loaf of bread.

Groups and Nulls

If a column that you are grouping by contains Null values, Access will create a single group for all the null values. This suggests that all the Null values are treated as being equal, which we have seen previously is not the case. The alternative would be to create a separate group (and therefore a separate row) for each individual Null value. In most cases this is not what you want. An example of how to do this using a Union query is provided in Unit 13.

Sorting and groups

In order to perform the grouping in a totals query, Access will sort the values in the group by columns. As a result the values in the data set returned by the query will be sorted, even though you have not specified any sort order. If you specify sorting on a column other than a column on which you are grouping, it may lead to poor performance. In some cases this may be inevitable – if you want to create a ranking you will need to sort by one of the columns being summarised, not a group by column.

Summarising data

Microsoft Access provides a number of aggregate functions that can be used for summarising data. These aggregate functions measure a characteristic of a set of values and return it as a single number. The sections below describe each function in detail.

Please note, the Access implementation of these aggregate functions differs from the same functions in other database products. It also differs from the definition of these functions in the international database standard called ISO SQL. This is mainly because the functions have been designed in such as way that they can be used not only in queries, but also for calculations in forms and reports.

Count

The Count function returns the number of known values in the particular column where it is used. The Count function will only count the row if it contains a known value; it will disregard any rows that contain Null values. If there are no non-Null values in the set of values, the function will return Null.

If you want to count every row in a table you can either count the Primary key column, which is guaranteed not to be Null, or you can type the expression Count(*) in the Field row of the query grid. Count(*) will count every row.

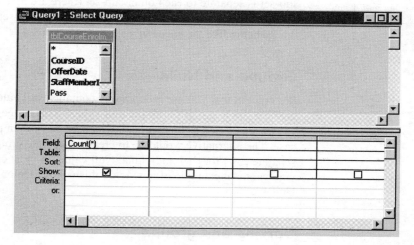

Fig 12.3
Using the expression Count(*) in a field of a query to return a count of all the rows in a table

Sum

The Sum function returns the numeric total of all the known values in a column. Null values are disregarded and the remaining values are added up. If there are no non-Null values the function will return Null. Sum only works with columns that have a numeric data type; if you try to use Sum on a text column, Access will generate an error message.

Using the sum function on columns involving real numbers may lead to rounding errors.

You should bear in mind that calculations involving real numbers (Single and Double field sizes) may suffer from rounding problems. For example, define a column in a table as a number with a Single field size. Enter two values into the column -10000.8 and -10000.7. Now create a totals query that sums the values in this column. You would expect to get a result of 0.1, but Access will actually return 0.99609375, which is close, but different enough to matter in some applications.

Avg

The Avg function returns the average of the known values in a column. If there are no non-Null values it will return Null. An average is a statistical function that provides a measure of central tendency. In fact, there are several averages. The Avg function returns the arithmetic mean of the values in a column. Access does not provide functions for calculating the median or the mode.

The Avg function disregards the Null values in the column. For this reason the result returned by Avg may not be the same as the result of an expression that divides the sum of the values in the column by the value returned by Count(*). The Sum function will disregard the Nulls whereas Count(*) will not.

Min and Max

The Min function returns the smallest known value in a column while the Max function returns the largest known value in a column. If there are no non-Null values, both functions will return Null. The functions work with Number, Text and Date/Time values. The way the functions work with numbers is what common sense would suggest. With Text values the Max function will return the last value when sorted in ascending alphabetic order while the Min function will return the first value when sorted in ascending alphabetic order.

When applied to a Date/Time column, the Max function will return the latest date and time in the set of values in the column, not the value that is closest to the current date. The Min function will return the earliest date and time.

First and Last

The First and Last functions are not part of the ANSI SQL standard and do not work as most people would expect. If you have sorted a table you would probably expect the First function to return the First value in the column according to the sort order that has been defined. In fact it does not. First will return the first value according to the physical ordering of rows in the table; Last will return the last value according to the physical ordering of rows in the table.

The First and Last functions do not work as most people would expect and are best avoided.

This breaks one of the fundamental rules of relational databases that holds that the physical ordering of the rows in a table is of no consequence to the operations of the data manipulation language. It also means that a query that uses these functions can give completely different results if the ordering of the records in the table change.

StdDev and Var

The standard deviation is a measure of dispersion and it measures the variation of values around the arithmetic mean. A small standard deviation means that the other values in the column are close to the arithmetic mean. Variance is the standard deviation squared. If you need to calculate descriptive statistics these functions can very useful, but further discussion is beyond the scope of this book.

Criteria and groups

You can specify criteria for a totals query in the same way as for other queries. If you apply criteria to a grouped column, or one that is being summarised using an aggregate function, Access will perform the grouping and summarising first and then compare the calculated values against the criteria. For example, the query in Figure 12.4 will return the names of departments that have more than 20 employees.

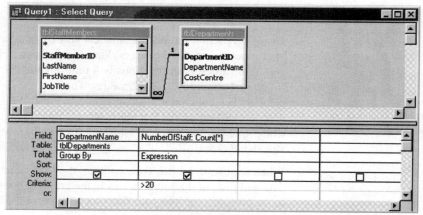

Fig 12.4
In this query Access will apply the criteria after the grouping and summarising is performed

Sometimes you need to be able to apply criteria before the aggregation occurs. For example, you might want to know how many clerks there are in each department. To do this you need to be able to filter the records first to find only those that have the word clerk somewhere in their job title. You can force Access to apply the criteria before aggregation by selecting Where in the Total row in the query grid:

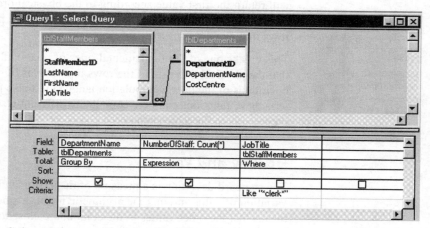

Fig 12.5
By choosing Where in the Total row you can force Access to apply criteria before the grouping and sorting are performed

Columns that are filtered using Where in the Total row do not appear in the datasheet that results from running the query. This is to ensure that the values in the column do not change the grouping and aggregation of the data.

You can apply criteria both before and after grouping. For example, if you wanted to find which departments had more than two clerks you would add the criteria >2 under the NumberOfStaff column to this query.

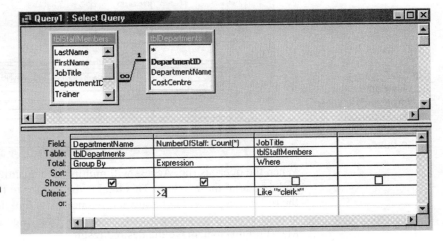

Fig 12.6
This query applies the criteria against the job title column before grouping, then the criteria against the count column after grouping

Applying criteria before grouping will usually provide better performance.

Some queries will give the same result irrespective of whether the criteria are applied before grouping or after grouping. If this is the case, the query will usually run faster if you apply the criteria before grouping using Where in the Totals row. In some cases you may have to include the same column twice in the query; once to group by and once more to specify the criteria with Where.

Calculated fields in totals queries

Access allows you to perform aggregation on calculated values. To apply the aggregation to a calculated column, enter the appropriate expression in the Field row in the query grid and then choose the appropriate aggregate function. On occasions you may also need to perform calculations using aggregated values.

For example, in an order processing system you may need to calculate the total value of each order including freight. To do this you may first need to calculate the extended value of each item on the order (by multiplying the quantity ordered by the unit price), total these amounts and then add to it the freight charge. In this case it is necessary to specify the aggregate functions in the expression in the Field row of the query grid and to select Expression in the Total row. Figure 12.7 uses the Orders sample database that is supplied with Access.

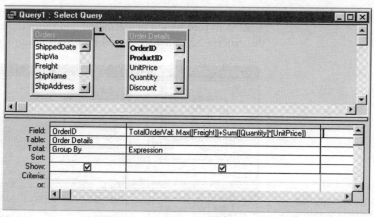

Fig 12.7
Access can
summarise calculated
values to perform
complex calculations
in the query

When the query is run, Access will multiply the quantity by the unit price
and then total these values. This total is then added to the freight charge for
the order. Access will not allow a reference to an individual column in this
kind of expression, so the Max function has been used in the expression
Max(Freight) to achieve the desired result.

Revision exercises

1. Using the Count function on a particular column may give a different result to
   using the expression Count(*). Why is this?

2. Why is it not possible to update the data returned by a totals query?

3. What will you find by using the Min function on a date column?

4. How do you force Access to apply criteria before grouping is performed in a totals
   query?

13 Advanced queries

What you will learn in this unit

This unit describes how to use the advanced queries provided by Microsoft Access. These include action queries that can change data and queries that need to be written using Structured Query Language (SQL). At the end of this unit you should:

❏ understand the various types of action query that can be used to alter data in the database

❏ be able to create an action query

❏ understand that some types of queries cannot be represented in the Query By Example (QBE) window and need to be written in SQL

❏ understand that SQL can also be used to retrieve data from other database products.

Queries that change data

The queries that we have looked at so far all select rows from the table or tables on which they are based. When those queries were run the selected rows are displayed in a datasheet. As outlined in Unit 11, queries that return rows like this are called 'select queries'. Access also provides the ability to create queries that change the data in the table or tables on which the query is based. These queries are known as 'action queries'.

Action queries provide a powerful way to manipulate data in your database. In many other products the only way to perform bulk updates of this kind is to write programs that change the data in the database tables.

You use action queries when you want to make changes to more than one row of data at the same time. For example, an external course provider may have increased their prices by 5 per cent. You could use an action query to increase the prices for courses offered by that course provider by the required 5 per cent. You can also use an action query to delete rows from an existing table, to append rows to an existing table, or to create a completely new table.

When you save an action query, Access will indicate that it is an action query by displaying a special icon next to the name of the query in the database window.

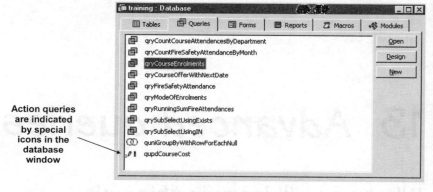

Fig 13.1
Different icons in the database window indicate the various queries

Action queries are indicated by special icons in the database window

If you run an action query from the database window, Access will display a message box advising that the action query will change data and asking you to confirm that you want to run the query.

Creating an action query

The safest way to create an action query is to create a select query first based on the same tables and using the same criteria. You can then run this query to make sure that it returns the rows that you expect. These are the rows that will be changed (or deleted) when you convert the query to an action query.

When you are sure that you have specified the correct criteria to select the records that you want to change, you can convert this select query to an action query. To do this you need to carry out the following.

1. In the Query design view click on the Query menu.

2. Choose the type of action query that you require.

Depending on the type of action query that you have selected, you may have to provide further information. This is described in the sections that follow.

Update queries

An update query changes data in records that already exist in a table.

You can use an update query to change the values held in one or more columns in one or more rows in an existing table. In the example given previously, an external course provider may have increased their prices by 5 per cent. You could update each record for this supplier by hand, however this would be both laborious and error prone. A better method would be to use an update query to update the required rows in one go.

To create an update query, follow these steps.

1. Create a select query that includes the necessary criteria to return the rows that you want to update. Ensure that the column or columns that you want to update are included in the query.

2. In Design View click on the Query menu and choose Update. Access will add an extra row labelled 'Update To:' in the grid in the bottom part of the Query design window.

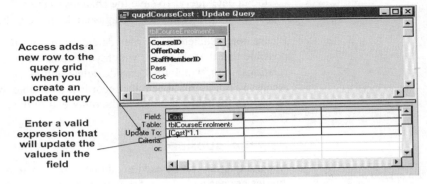

Fig 13.2
Using an update query to change existing records in a table

3. Enter a valid expression that will make the necessary changes. The value in the column will be changed to the value that is returned by the expression.

4. To run the query, click on the Query menu and choose Run (or click on the Run button on the Query design toolbar). Access will display a message box advising you of the number of rows that will be affected by the update query. To save the changes to the affected rows, click on the OK button. To undo the changes click on the Cancel button.

Please note, if you click on the datasheet button on the Query design toolbar for an update query, Access will display a datasheet containing the columns in the table that will be updated. No rows will be updated. You should be aware that the values that you see are the current values and not the new values that the rows will contain after the update query is run. This can be a source of confusion.

Delete queries

A delete query deletes records from a table.

Delete queries can be used to delete all the rows in a particular table, or a group of rows that meet particular criteria. For example, you may want to delete all records of course attendance more that one year prior to the current date.

To create the delete query, follow these steps.

1. Create a select query that includes the necessary criteria to return the rows that you want to update. Drag the asterisk to the query grid from the field list for the table from which you want to delete rows.

2. In Design View click on the Query menu and choose Delete. Access will add an extra row labelled 'Delete:' in the grid in the bottom part of the Query design window.

3. To run the query, click on the Query menu and choose Run (or click on the Run button on the Query design toolbar). Access will display a message box advising you of the number of rows that will be affected by the update query. To save the changes to the affected rows click on the OK button. To undo the changes click on the Cancel button.

Please note, a delete query may delete more rows than you expect. It is possible that the table from which you are deleting is on the one side of a relationship on which the Cascade delete option has been set. In this case Access will not only delete the records in this table, but also all related records in the table or tables at the other end of the relationship.

Append queries

An append query adds new records to a table that already exists.

Append queries can be used to add new rows to an existing table. Append queries are particularly useful when importing data from other sources. The data to be imported is rarely in the same format as the database design. In this case the data can be imported into a temporary table that follows the existing structure of the data, then one or more append queries can select the required data and append to the appropriate tables in the database.

To create an append query, follow these steps.

1. Create a select query that includes the necessary criteria to return the rows that you want to append to an existing table.

2. In Design View click on the Query menu and choose Append. Access will display the following dialogue box to enable you to choose the table to which the rows will be appended.

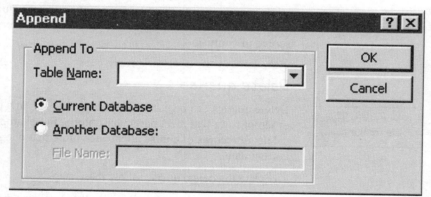

Fig 13.3
Selecting the table to which records will be added by an append query

3. When you have selected the required table, click on the OK button. Access will add an extra row labelled 'Append:' in the grid in the bottom part of the Query design window. If any of the field names in the query match the field names in the destination table, Access will automatically insert the name in the Append To row in the query grid. If the destination field name does not appear automatically, you must select the destination field from the list that drops down from the Append To row.

4. To run the query, click on the Query menu and choose Run (or click on the Run button on the Query design toolbar). Access will display a message box advising you of the number of rows that will be appended to the existing table. To save the changes to the affected rows, click on the OK button. To undo the changes, click on the Cancel button.

Make table queries

A make table inserts records into a completely new table in the database.

Make table queries can be used to create a completely new table using values in an existing table. Make table queries can be useful if you want to archive your data into separate tables for different time intervals. For example, in a large database you may have one table containing current transactions and separate tables each containing a different month's data.

You can also use make table queries to create temporary tables. In some cases a complicated query can run very slowly if it has to process a large amount of data. These queries can run much faster if data is filtered first and stored in a temporary table, and the results are then constructed from the data stored in the temporary table.

To create a make table query, follow these steps.

1. Create a select query that includes the necessary criteria to return the rows that you want to copy into a new table.

2. In Design View click on the Query menu and choose Make Table. Access will display the following dialogue box to enable you to choose the name of the table that will be created.

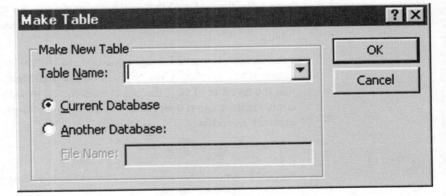

Fig 13.4
Naming the table that will be created by a Make Table query

3. To run the query click on the Query menu and choose Run (or click on the Run button on the Query design toolbar). Access will display a message box advising you of the number of rows that will be appended to the existing table. To save the changes to the affected rows, click on the OK button. To undo the changes, click on the Cancel button.

SQL-specific queries

When you create a query using the Query design window, Access automatically converts your actions to a programming language called Structured Query Language or SQL (pronounced either as ess-que-ell or sequel). When you save the query, Access saves the SQL. When you open a saved query in Design View, Access converts the saved SQL into its graphical representation in the Query design window. To view the SQL that is created by the Query design window, click on the SQL button on the Query design toolbar.

In many products, writing SQL statements is the only way to retrieve data from the database.

SQL is the most commonly used data definition and data manipulation language. You can find SQL in use in database products that run on PCs (such as Microsoft Access and FoxPro), on mini computers (products such as Oracle, Ingres and Informix), and on mainframe computers (in products such as IBM's DB2).

A detailed discussion of SQL is beyond the scope of this book. In most cases in Access it is not necessary to write SQL – the Query design window handles that task for you. However, there are some specific cases where the Query design window cannot create the query for you and you will have to resort to writing SQL yourself.

Union queries

A union query returns records from more than one table without performing a join.

A Union query combines the rows in two or more tables, or two or more queries. Whereas a standard select query that is based on more than one table joins the tables so that you get a single row for each matching row in the tables, a union query returns a separate row for each row in the different tables.

For example, if we had created one table to hold information about external course tutors and had a Yes/No field on the StaffMembers table to indicate that the member of staff teaches classes for us, to see a list of all tutors we could create a union query that will show us all tutors, both internal and external, as follows.

```
TABLE ExternalTutors
UNION
SELECT StaffMemberID, FirstName, LastName
FROM StaffMembers
WHERE CourseTutor = True
```

This query would produce a row for each row in the ExternalTutors table, as well as a row for each member of staff flagged as being a course tutor in the StaffMembers table.

In cases where there are duplicate rows in both tables, Access will return only a single row for the duplicates. If you do not want this to happen, you must specify the ALL keyword, as follows.

```
TABLE ExternalTutors
UNION ALL
SELECT StaffMemberID, FirstName, LastName
FROM StaffMembers
WHERE CourseTutor = True
```

Please note, all Union queries are read-only. You cannot update values in a datasheet returned from a union query.

Creating a union query

The designers of Microsoft Access were unable to come up with a way to represent union queries in the Query design grid. The only way to create a query is to write (or copy) the necessary SQL statements. To create a union query, follow these steps.

1. Create a new query, but do not select any tables to add to the query. Just close the Add table dialogue.

2. In Query design view, click on the Query menu and choose SQL specific. A sub-menu will appear. Choose union from the sub-menu.

3. The Query design window will change to a blank white document where you can type in the SQL for the query.

If you find the blank window intimidating, you can make life easier by designing separate queries for the different parts of the union. When you have created these queries, switch to SQL view of the query and cut and paste the SQL generated by the Query design window into the SQL view of the union query.

Sorting a union query

If you want to sort the results of a union query you must specify the sort of the last query in the union. Access ignores a sort on any query in the union other than the last. The sort order that you choose in the Query design window translates to an Order By clause in SQL. Thus, if we wanted to sort the union of the course tutors by last name we would specify the SQL as follows.

```
TABLE ExternalTutors
UNION ALL
SELECT StaffMemberID, FirstName, LastName
FROM StaffMembers
WHERE CourseTutor = True
ORDER BY LastName
```

Rules for union queries

You can create a union between two tables or two queries provided that each table or query contains the same number of columns. These columns do not have to have the same name or even the same data type. If they do not, Access follows these rules.

- If the columns have different names, Access uses the names from the first table or query.

- If the columns have different data types, Access will convert the column to a data type that is compatible with all values. For example, if you union an integer column with a double column, Access will convert the column to a double. Text combined with a number will produce text, dates combined with text will produce text, and so on.

- You cannot use memo columns or OLE object columns in union queries.

Other examples of union queries

A union query can be used to create rows for values that do not exist in a table.

Union queries can be useful for adding dynamic values to values that are selected from a table or query. For example, a common requirement is to add a row with the word 'All' to a list of values that can be selected from a list box or combo box. This can be achieved using a union query, as follows.

```
SELECT '*' as CourseID, '<All>' as CourseTitle
FROM tblCourses
UNION
SELECT CourseID, CourseTitle
FROM tblCourses
ORDER BY CourseTitle
```

As mentioned in Unit 12, you can also use the union operator to create a totals query that returns each separate row that contains a Null value in a column that you are grouping by, together with a row for each group containing a non-Null value. The following query will return a row for each cost centre in the Departments table with the departments in that cost centre, plus a row for each department where the cost centre is Null together with the name of that department.

```
SELECT CostCentre, DepartmentName
FROM tblDepartments
WHERE CostCentre Is Null
UNION
SELECT CostCentre, Count(*)
FROM tblDepartments
GROUP BY CostCentre
HAVING CostCentre Is Not Null
```

Other SQL specific queries

Access allows you to create queries that contain other queries by typing a valid SQL statement into the criteria row of the QBE grid. This type of query is known as a 'sub-select query'. It is also possible to type a valid SQL statement into the field row of the query grid. This type of query is called a 'correlated sub-query'. These advanced queries are beyond the scope of this book.

Revision exercises

1. All employees have been awarded a 5 per cent pay rise. What type of query would you use to change the values held in an employees table?

2. You are required to delete all the orders in an Orders table that are more than 5 years old. The table contains a field called OrderDate that holds the date of the order. How would you achieve this using a query?

3. You have been provided with a spreadsheet that contains information about new employees. The structure of the spreadsheet is the same as the table in the database. How would you get this data into the Employees table?

14 Presenting information using reports

What you will learn in this unit

This unit describes how to use reports to present the information that is derived from the data in your database. At the end of this unit you should:

❑ understand the various types of report that can be used to present information

❑ understand the parts of a report

❑ be able to customise an existing report

❑ understand the sorting and grouping options offered by an Access report.

Why use a report?

Forms and reports in Access are closely related. You can create a form design and then ask Access to save that design as a report.

Reports, like forms, enable you to present your data how you want. However, reports differ from forms in that they do not provide a means to alter data. Reports are designed primarily to present information in a printed format, although they can be previewed on screen before printing. Access reports are What You See Is What You Get (WYSIWYG). With a report you can:

• group and sort the data in the report

• do calculations on the data in the report

• show data from more than one table using sub-reports

• display graphs and images

For more information about creating queries based on more than one table, see Unit 11.

• present information in an appealing way using graphical devices such a lines, shading and colours.

Most reports are based on queries. In a fully normalised database the main tables will hold codes or numbers in a lot of columns. The meanings of these codes will be held in separate tables, usually called lookup tables. Before you can start to create a report you will usually have to construct a query that combines the main tables with lookup tables to enable the report to display meaningful values instead of codes.

Types of report

Access provides a number of different types of report. The two most basic types are columnar reports and tabular reports. In a columnar report the fields in the table or query on which the report is based are arranged in a single column down the length of the report. Columnar reports are usually printed in landscape format.

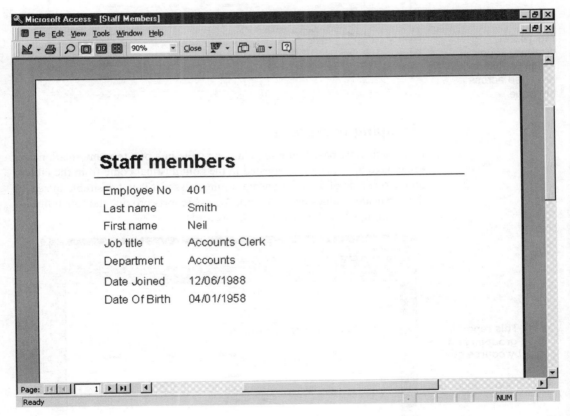

Fig 14.1
A columnar report in which fields are arranged down the length of the page

In a tabular report the fields in the table or query on which the report is based are arranged across the page. Each record has a line to itself on the report and each field has its own column on the report.

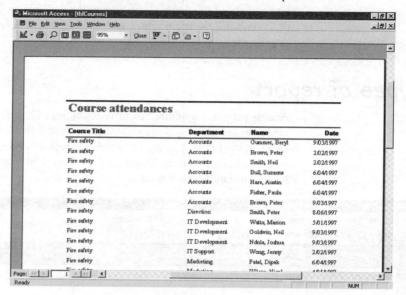

Fig 14.2
A tabular report in which fields are arranged across the page

Grouping in reports

Queries that are based on more than one table in a one-to-many relationship often have the same data repeated in the columns that come from the table on the one side of the relationship. In most cases it is not desirable to see these repeated values on the report. Access reports provide the capability to define groups based on values in the records.

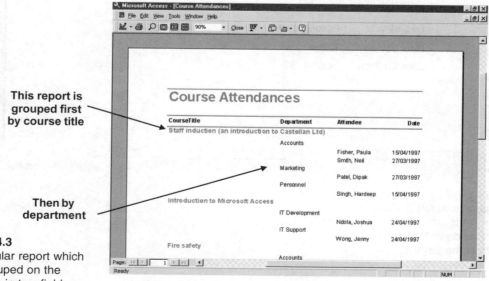

This report is grouped first by course title

Then by department

Fig 14.3
A tabular report which is grouped on the values in two fields

Access provides the capability to show sub-totals and other summarised values for each group in a report, and for the report as a whole.

By choosing to group the report on a field that contains repeating values, you can ensure that the value is shown only once on the report. This also ensures that all the records for that group are shown together on the report.

Understanding the reports created by the wizard

Creating a report from scratch can be very laborious. Access provides a number of report wizards that can help you to do most of the tedious work that is involved in creating a report. Even if you don't like the layout or format produced by the wizard, you can use them as a starting point that you can modify after the wizard has finished.

Access offers many different types of wizards as well as a sort of instant wizard called Auto Report. The following is a summary of the type of report that each wizard will produce.

- **Auto Report columnar** – creates a report in which the data fields are arranged in a column that stretches down the length of the report.

- **Auto Report tabular** – creates a report in which the data fields are arranged across the width of the page. This wizard may automatically group one or more fields in the report.

- **Report wizard** – creates a report that is arranged in a tabular format, but you can choose the grouping for the report. Each group that is displayed on the report can also show sub-totals for each group. In addition it can show grand totals for all the records that are contained in the report.

- **Label wizard** – creates a report that is designed to fit the information that is displayed into a format that can be printed on mailing label stationery.

Running the report

When you run a report, Access will usually display it first in Print Preview mode. In Print Preview you can view the report as it will appear when printed. The Preview window has a set of navigation buttons that let you move through the report. Unlike the buttons on a form window which move one record at a time, the navigation buttons on a report window move through the report one page at a time.

Clicking on the report in the Print Preview window will change the zoom level so that you can see less of the page but in more detail, or the whole page in less detail. You can control the zoom level more precisely using the zoom combo box on the Report Preview toolbar.

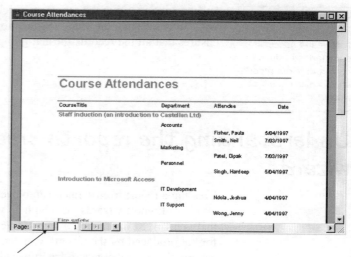

Fig 14.4
A report shown in a
Print Preview window

Use these buttons to navigate through the
pages of the report

Layout View produces a
preview of the report
using sample data
instead of the real data.

If the report is complicated, it may take some time to run. If you are in the
process of designing the report, you may be more interested in seeing the
appearance of the layout rather than the data values that are being
calculated. If this is the case you can open the report in Layout View.

Changing the report design

Print Preview and Layout View allow you to run the report to see how it
will appear when it is printed. However, you cannot change the design on
the report in Print Preview mode. In order to change the design of a report
you must open it in Design View.

A report is arranged in sections and these sections contain controls, just like
a form. You work with the controls and sections on a report in exactly the
same way as you work with a form. The toolbox, the field list and the
various options on the Report design toolbar are available for working with
the report design.

Because the sections
on a report appear as
bands in Design View,
Access is sometimes
referred to as a
'banded' report writer.

A simple report can have the same sections as a form; there may be a report
header and report footer, a page header and a page footer, plus a detail
section. A more complicated report that performs grouping may have an
additional header and footer section for each of the fields that are used for
grouping. Figure 14.5 is the same report as the previous figure, but shown in
Design View.

Fig 14.5
A tabular report in Design View. The report design has many sections that appear as bands in the design

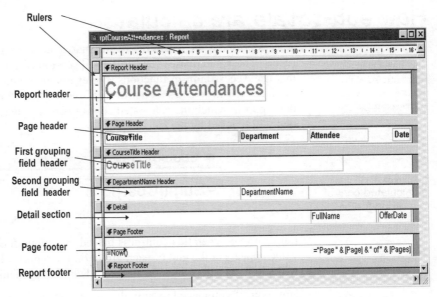

The section of the report in which the control is located determines how many times a field's value is displayed on a report.

- **Report header** – anything in this section of the report will only appear once at the top of the first page of the report.

- **Page header** – anything in this section of the report will appear at the top of every page of the report.

- **Grouping field headers** – each field on which you are grouping can have its own header. Anything in a grouping field header will appear once for each distinct value in the field on which the grouping is performed. In Figure 14.4, each individual Course title only appears once, even though the value may be duplicated many times in the query on which the report is based.

- **Detail** – any fields in this section will appear once for every record in the table or query on which the report is based.

- **Grouping field footers** – each field on which you are grouping can have its own footer. Anything in a grouping field footer will appear once for each distinct value in the field on which the grouping is performed.

- **Page footer** – anything in this section of the report will appear at the bottom of each page of the report.

- **Report footer** – anything in this section of the report will appear at the bottom of the last page of the report.

How sub-totals are calculated

For more information about the built-in functions available in Access, see Appendix A on using expressions.

Access provides the capability to summarise data from each section in a report. These summaries (usually called sub-totals) are calculated in controls that use Access built-in functions. For example, to add up all the values in a field, the wizard creates a control that uses the Sum function. The section of the report in which the calculated control is placed determines the records that will be used by the calculation.

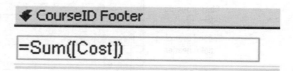

Fig 14.6
A calculated control in a group footer

For example, when this control is placed in a group footer the calculated value appears at the end of each group on the report. The calculated control will add up all the values for the records in that particular group only.

However, if you placed exactly the same control in the Report footer section it would add up the values in that field in the entire report. You would see the total only once at the end of the report.

Formatting the report

As mentioned previously, you can use the same tools and techniques for formatting reports as you use for formatting forms. In the same way as for forms, every section and every control on the report has its own set of properties. These properties can be used to alter the appearance and formatting of the information that is displayed on the report.

Setting the display format for a control

Often you will want to alter the way data from a table is presented on a report. For example, you may want to show a date in a particular way, or format currency values to a certain number of decimal places. You do this using the format property for a control.

You alter the formatting of a report in Design View. To change the format of a particular control, double-click on the control so that the Properties window is showing. In the Properties window, select the Format property. A button with a down arrow will appear next to the Format property row. Click on the down arrow to see a list of common formats.

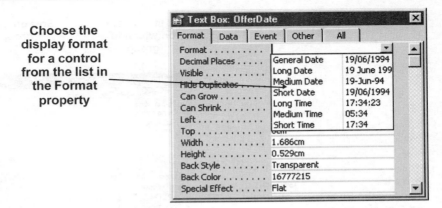

Choose the display format for a control from the list in the Format property

Fig 14.7
Changing the Format property for a control

You can also enter more specific formatting options directly into the Properties window. You can get more information on format settings by clicking on the Format property in the Properties window and then pressing the F1 key on the keyboard to display the Help topic.

Other useful formatting properties

*   **Can grow and Can shrink** – the values in these properties determine whether a control on a report can shrink if there is no data in the underlying record or grow larger to accommodate larger amounts of text in the underlying record. If you find that a control on a report is not big enough to display all the data in a record, set the Can grow property to Yes. The control will resize to fit the amount of text in each record.

*   **Hide duplicates** – if this property is set to Yes, the control will not be displayed on the report if the current record contains the same value in this field as the previous record.

*   **Running sum** – if this property is set to True the control will accumulate and display a running sum of the values in the bound field, instead of each individual value. You can show a running sum for the whole report or for each group on a report.

Changing sorting and grouping

If you are going to sort the values in a report there is little point sorting values in the query on which the report is based.

You can determine how the values on a report are sorted and grouped using the Sorting and Grouping window. To show the Sorting and Grouping window, click on the View menu and choose Sorting and Grouping, or click on the Sorting and Grouping button on the Report design toolbar.

The Sorting and Grouping box is shown Fig 14.8. The top part is a grid in which you select the fields by which you want to sort or group items in the report and set the Sort Order. The bottom part sets options for grouping.

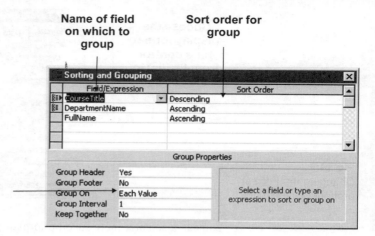

Name of field on which to group

Sort order for group

Fig 14.8
Changing the Sorting and Grouping on a report

Grouping options

Adding more groups to the report

To add more groups to the report, click on the next available Field/Expression cell in the Sorting and Grouping dialogue box. A drop down list of available fields will appear. Choose the field for which you want to create the group.

Changing the Sorting and Grouping order

The order in which the fields appear in the grid in the Sorting and Grouping box controls the order in which the groups appear on the report. To change this order, follow these two steps.

1. Click on the row selector button next to the field in the grid.

2. Drag on the row selector button to move the row to the required position.

Deleting a field from the Sorting and Grouping box

To delete a field from the Sorting and Grouping box, follow these two steps.

1. Click on the row selector button next to the field in the grid.

2. Press the delete key on the keyboard.

Grouping options

The following options determine grouping on the report and can be set for up to 10 fields in the report.

- **Group header** – determines whether a header section is created on the report for the grouping field. If set to Yes, Access will create a group header section on the report for the grouping field.

- **Group footer** – determines whether a footer section is created on the report for the grouping field. If set to Yes, Access will create a group footer section on the report for the grouping field.

- **Group on** – specifies how you want the values grouped. The options you see depend on the data type of the field on which you are grouping. If you are grouping on a text value, you will usually have the option of grouping on each value or on prefix characters (for example, you may want to group on the first letter of a surname when producing a telephone directory). If you are grouping on a Date/Time field, you will be able to group on parts of a date, such as the day, month or year, or on aggregations such as weeks or quarters.

- **Group interval** – specifies number to qualify the grouping. For example, if you have chosen to group on prefix characters, type 1 here to specify that you want to group on the first character, 2 to group on the first two characters, and so on.

- **Keep together** – determines whether Microsoft Access prints all or only part of a group on one page. The following options are available:

  No – (Default) prints the group without keeping the group header, detail section, and group footer on the same page

  Whole Group – prints the group header, detail section and group footer on the same page

  With First Detail – prints the group header on a page only if it can also print the first detail record that goes with it.

Creating a Main-report/Sub-report combination

A report can show related records from another table or query in a sub-report in the same way as for a form. You can create a Main-report/Sub-report combination using the wizard in exactly the same way as you create a sub-form.

Showing page numbers on a report

A report has some special properties that can be used to enhance the appearance of the report. The Page property returns the number of the current page of the report. The Pages property returns the total number of pages on the report. You may see a text box on a report created by the wizard that looks like the following.

Fig 14.9
Showing page
numbers on a report

="Page " & [Page] & " of" & [Pages]

This expression calculates the current page number and total number of pages, and displays it in the format "Page 1 of 5".

Reports that show the total number of pages can run extremely slowly because Access has to calculate this total before it even starts formatting the first page.

Revision exercises

1. List the purposes for which a tabular report is most appropriate and the purposes for which a columnar report is better suited.

2. Why are most reports based on queries rather than the base tables in a database?

3. What is the purpose of grouping in a report?

4. When computerisation became common in organisations, many people predicted the coming of the 'paperless office'. So far, history has proved them wrong. Discuss the reasons why printed reports are still so widely used in a business environment.

15 Presenting information graphically using charts

What you will learn in this unit

This unit describes how to present information in a graphical format using charts.

At the end of this unit you should:

- ❑ appreciate that quantitative information can be more easily understood if it is presented visually

- ❑ recognise that the presentation of quantitative information should be truthful, understandable and explained

- ❑ understand the terminology used to describe the parts of a chart

- ❑ understand the different types of chart that are available, and the purposes that they serve

- ❑ understand how to customise a chart that has been created using the wizard.

Presenting information visually

Some types of systems, variously described as Decision Support Systems or Management Information Systems, make extensive use of charts to assist in the analysis and presentation of information.

Quantitative information is often more easily understood if it is presented visually. Our eyes are able to detect patterns and trends in information that is presented in a graphical form. These patterns may not be so apparent if the information is presented in a report that simply contains an arrangement of text and numbers.

The usual method for presenting information visually is a chart. We see charts all the time – in newspapers, magazines, books and on the television. In an organisation there is often a requirement for management reports to contain charts, or for a system to present graphical output on-line.

Although charts can be a valuable tool in presenting information, they have received a bad reputation in recent years. This is because charts have often been used to present biased or misleading information. In some cases this is done deliberately leading to the belief that it is possible to prove anything with statistics. More often these days, it can be the result of a failure to understand the basic principles of presenting information visually. When designing a chart you should ensure that it meets the following criteria.

- **Does it tell the truth?** Any chart must present a truthful representation of the data that it contains. A chart can be made misleading by simply 'massaging' the underlying data on which it is based. This massaging may take the form of excessive selectivity or out and out fabrication.

- **Can it be understood?** The 'keep it simple' principle applies to charts. There is always a temptation to present more and more data on a chart. Since the main reason for presenting information on a chart is to help see the wood for the trees, overloading a chart with more and more data is counter-productive. However, you should ensure that you do not distort the picture presented by the chart by omitting relevant information.

- **Is it explained?** Even if the chart is simple, it must be easy to work out what it represents. You should ensure that the various elements of the chart are clearly labelled and that scales are represented accurately. A chart should also have a title that explains what is being presented. When the chart is displayed in a form or report, you may have to include some additional text in a label or text box that further explains what is presented in the chart.

The parts of a chart

There are a number of technical terms that apply to charts. The diagram below shows the names of the various parts of a bar chart.

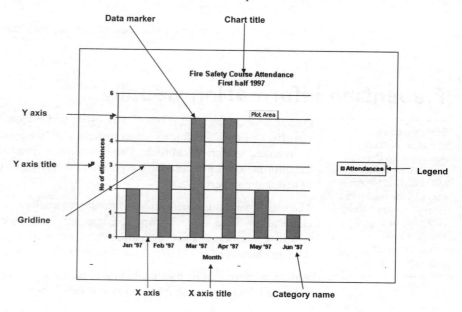

Fig 15.1
The parts of a bar chart

Choosing the correct type of chart

Access provides many different types of chart to display information. It is important to know which chart is appropriate for a given situation.

Chart type	Description
Pie chart	Pie charts are used to show proportions of components to the whole. While they are not suitable for presenting precise numerical data, they can provide a better view of the relative importance of components than viewing the numbers themselves.
	The most important consideration when using a pie chart is to ensure that the entire population that is being portrayed is included in the data on which the chart is based. A pie chart is not a suitable tool if we cannot accurately represent the whole. For example, if we wanted to present demographic information for the whole of the country, we would need to ensure that no data was missing.
Doughnut charts	Doughnut charts are similar to pie charts but allow you to show more than one set of values. Each set of values is represented in a separate ring of the doughnut. Doughnut charts can be extremely difficult to read. The fact that the rings are concentric makes it difficult to see the relative proportions of the slices in different rings. Two separate pie charts are often easier to understand than two data series on a single doughnut chart.
Bar charts	Bar charts are often used to represent the magnitude of the individual components. Each bar can represent a different grouping of values or a time value (such as a separate bar for each month or year). The bars in the chart can run horizontally or vertically (a bar chart with vertical columns is called a column chart).
Histogram	A histogram is a specialised type of column chart that shows a frequency distribution of a particular value. The data is partitioned into equally sized groups that are shown in a continuous range. The chart must show the entire range and there should be no gaps in the values. In a histogram the columns are usually the same width and are arranged so that there is no physical gap between them on the chart.
Line charts	Line charts can be used to display the same kind of data as a bar chart, but are more useful for identifying trends in the data. For this reason, line charts are often used to display the changes in a value over time. Lines can also be used to show cumulative figures.

| Combination charts | Access will allow you to create mixed charts combining a number of these chart types. The most common combination of chart types is a column chart showing one set of values and a line chart showing a different set of values. |
| Other charts | Access also provides the capability to produce other charts such as scatter diagrams and area charts. If the intended audience has training in statistics and is familiar with this type of chart, they can be useful in an appropriate situation. However, these types of chart are not really suitable for a general audience. |

Creating a chart using the wizard

In almost all cases a chart will be based on the results of a query rather than on the whole table. The first step to creating a chart is to create the query that will provide the appropriate data.

You can create a chart for display on a form or on a report. The process is effectively the same in both cases. You can either create a chart that takes up the whole of a new form or report, or insert a chart on an existing form or report.

To create a new form or report to display a chart, follow these steps.

1. Click on the form or report tab (as appropriate) in the database window.

2. Click on the New button. In the New report dialogue box, choose Chart Wizard from the list of options.

3. Select the query that will provide the data to your chart from the combo box labelled 'Choose the table or query...'. Now click on the OK button. Follow the steps in the wizard.

To insert a new chart on an existing form or report, follow these steps.

1. Open the form or report in Design View.

2. Click on the Insert menu and choose Chart. The mouse pointer will change to a small chart icon. Click and drag on the surface of the form to draw a rectangle to mark the position where the chart will be inserted.

3. When you let go of the mouse button the chart wizard will start. Follow the steps in the wizard.

Customising a chart created by the wizard

The wizard will create a chart according to the selections that you make, as well as the values that have been pre-set by the developers at Microsoft. Unfortunately, some essential items (such as X and Y axis labels) are missing from the charts created by the wizard. However, you can edit the charts created by the wizard to ensure that they appear as you require.

Before looking at how to modify a chart, it is important to realise that Access itself has no ability to create charts. The charts that appear in an Access database are actually created by another application (that is supplied with Access), called Microsoft Graph. Access communicates with Graph using a technology called Object Linking and Embedding (OLE – usually pronounced 'oh lay').

Modifying the properties of the chart control

When you create a chart on a form or report, Access creates a special control on the form or report to hold the OLE object. This control has a set of properties in the same way as other controls. For example, the Row Source property controls the source from which the data is drawn for the chart. If the chart does not show the data that you require, you may be able to change the value held in this property (using the Query design window that pops up when you click on the button with the ellipsis).

One property that you will probably want to change is the Size mode property. The wizard sets this property to 'Clip', which means that the control displays the chart in its actual size. If you want the chart to re-size to fill the size of the control, you should change this property to 'Stretch'. To find out more information about other properties, select the property in the properties window and then press the F1 key.

Modifying the chart object

To change the appearance of the chart itself, click once on the chart object to select it and then double-click on it. Microsoft Graph will launch and appear in its own window over the top of the Access window.

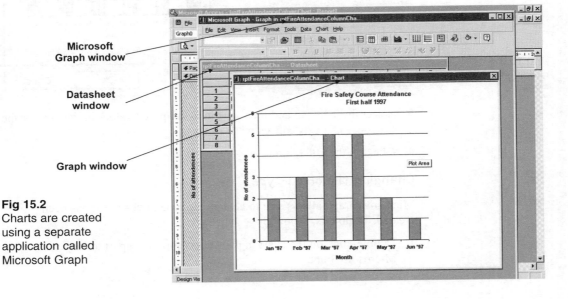

Microsoft Graph window

Datasheet window

Graph window

Fig 15.2
Charts are created using a separate application called Microsoft Graph

The Microsoft Graph application contains two document windows – one is a datasheet and the other contains the chart itself. The datasheet window serves no purpose in an Access chart since the data is drawn dynamically from a query rather than from static values in the datasheet. The chart window can be used to modify the appearance of the chart.

When you have completed modifying a chart you return to Microsoft Access by clicking on the File menu (make sure you are clicking on the menus in the Microsoft Graph window – it is easy to click on the Access window that is behind), then choose Exit and Return to Microsoft Access.

Adding X and Y axis titles to the chart

To add X and Y axis to a chart, follow these steps.

1. Double-click on the chart in the Access form or report to launch Microsoft Graph.

2. Make sure that the chart window is selected. Click on the Chart menu and choose Chart Options. You will see the following dialogue.

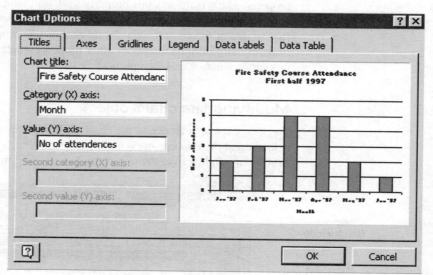

Fig 15.3
Adding titles to a chart

3. Select the Title tab and then type in the required values in the box for the Category (X) axis and Value (Y) axis.

4. Click on the OK button.

Changing the chart type

Microsoft Graph allows you to change the type of chart that has been created. To do this, follow these steps.

1. Double-click on the chart in the Access form or report to launch Microsoft Graph.

2. Make sure that the Chart window is selected, then click on the Chart menu and choose Chart Type. You will see the following dialogue.

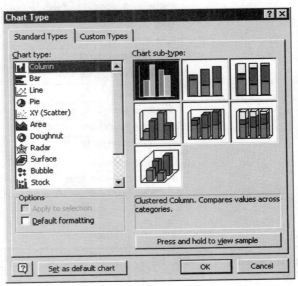

Fig 15.4
Changing the chart type

3. Choose the chart type that you require. You can select from a list of standard chart types or define your own custom chart types.

Changing individual parts of the chart

The process of clicking on an object once to select it and then double-clicking to edit it is a standard Windows technique.

You can change the appearance of almost all the elements in a chart. The procedure is the same. Click on the item to select it and then double-click on it to edit it. In some cases you will be able to edit the item in place; in other cases a dialogue box will appear to allow you to set the values concerned.

Changing chart text

You can change the chart titles and data labels by double clicking on them and editing in place. To change other text, double click on the item and then change the appropriate item in the dialogue box.

Changing the Y axis properties

In some cases the wizard may create a chart in which the Y axis does not originate at zero. You can change this as follows.

1. Double-click on the chart in the Access form or report to launch Microsoft Graph.

2. Click once on the Y axis line to select it and then double click on it. You will see the following dialogue box.

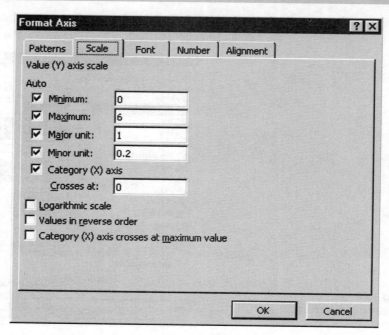

Fig 15.5
Changing the format
of a chart axis

3. Make sure that the text box labelled 'Minimum' is set to zero and then click on the OK button.

Revision exercises

1. Choose the most appropriate chart type for the following reports:

(a) a chart that shows the number of staff in each department for the whole organisation

(b) the number of people attending a course broken down by month

(c) a cumulative total for the number of people attending a course broken down by month.

2. Why should the scale for the Y axis on a chart always start from zero?

3. What titles can you show on a chart? What is the purpose of each one?

4. Charts are a common way of presenting misleading information. How is it possible to misrepresent data in a chart and how can this be avoided?

16 Optimising database performance

What you will learn in this unit

This unit describes how to alter the design of a database to improve performance. At the end of this unit you should:

❒ understand how the perception of poor performance can affect the usefulness and acceptance of a database system

❒ understand how indexes can be used to speed up data retrieval

❒ understand that indexing can also reduce performance and that an indexing strategy should be adopted for the particular circumstances of the database

❒ understand other techniques for improving the performance of an Access database.

Do relational databases have performance problems?

The people who made the most noise about the performance of relational databases were often those who saw their own products losing market share to the new relational products.

The first commercial database products to implement the relational model appeared in the late 1970s. At that time a number of people complained that the performance of these products was inferior to other products available at the time.

Claims that current database management systems based on the relational model are inherently slower than other products can no longer be sustained. However, it remains the case that it is easy to create a poorly designed database using a product such as Microsoft Access and the performance of the database will suffer as a result.

The first part of this book has looked at the methods that can be used to create a database design that is most appropriate for implementation in a relational database. This unit looks at specific techniques to optimise the performance of those databases.

Indexes to speed up data retrieval

An index in a database works in much the same way as an index in a book.

An index in a database works like an index in a book. If you wanted to find the location of an address that you had never been to, you would try and find it in a street directory. You could try looking at each map in turn and try to find the road you are looking for, but this could take some time. Instead you would find the name of the road in the index. The index would refer you to a page in the directory and to a grid reference on that page.

A database index works in the same way. If an index is created on a column in a table, the index will hold an entry for the values held in the table, plus a reference to the physical location on the disk where rows containing that value can be found.

Searching through every row in a table is called a 'full table scan' and can take a long time.

If you specify search criteria on a column that is not indexed, Access will be forced to load each row in the table into memory and examine each row to determine which rows match the criteria. If an index is created on the column against which the search criteria are specified, Access need only load the index into memory to determine which rows meet the criteria and then retrieve only those matching rows that are referenced in the index.

Indexes can increase the performance of searching and sorting operations and can dramatically improve the efficiency of queries that join multiple tables on Foreign key values. If the database resides on a file server in a networked environment, judicious use of indexes can also reduce the amount of network traffic generated by database activity.

Types of index

Primary key constraints are actually enforced by a unique index.

Access supports two types of index: unique indexes and non-unique indexes. By defining a unique index on a column, you are instructing Access to ensure that there will be no duplicate values in the column. In fact, this is how Access enforces the uniqueness of a Primary key, but you do not have to specify that you want the index on the Primary key; Access does this for you automatically.

In most cases when you need to create an index manually you will want a non-unique index, since this will allow duplicate values in the indexed column.

Which columns should you index?

Deciding which columns to index requires an understanding of the values that are likely to be held in the table concerned. Here are some general guidelines.

- Only consider indexing a column if its data type is Text, Number, Date/Time or Currency.

- Always index Foreign key columns. A non-unique index on a Foreign key column will improve the efficiency of queries that join multiple tables by several orders of magnitude. This is because Access will often be able to perform the join on the indexes themselves, thus reducing the number of actual rows that need to be retrieved by the query. Be aware that Access may automatically index a Foreign key column (see the section on Indexes that Access creates automatically below).

- Index a column if you will often be searching for particular values or a range of values in the column.

- Index a column if you will often be sorting the rows in the table according to the values in the column.

An index will not increase performance on a column that only holds one or two distinct values.

Whether the index will speed up queries will ultimately depend on the values held in the column. If the table contains many rows that contain the same value in the indexed column, Access may end up doing a full table scan anyway because the index is not varied enough to make it worth using. This is why there is no point indexing a column with a Yes/No data type. If more than 50 per cent of the rows in the table hold the same value in that column, you may not see any performance benefit at all from indexing the column.

Why not index every column?

An index will degrade performance on inserts and updates to the table.

If indexes can improve the performance of data retrieval so much, why not index everything? As with most things, there is no such thing as a free lunch. While an index can improve the performance of data retrieval, it can also slow down the process of inserting, updating and deleting rows.

This is because when you change the data in an indexed column, Access not only has to write the value back to the disk when it saves the record, it also has to update the index as well. Maintaining the index therefore increases the amount of disk activity (and possibly network traffic) when the data is updated.

Therefore you have to weigh up the pros and cons of creating the index. If your application is used for transaction processing and the speed with which the data can be entered or updated is a primary concern, too many indexes will have a negative impact on performance. If, on the other hand, your database is used mainly for performing on-line analysis on fairly static data, indexing columns used for searching and sorting should improve performance.

Creating an index in Access

The way that you create an index in Access differs depending on whether you are indexing a single field or multiple fields.

Creating an index on a single field

The Indexed field property determines whether an individual field is indexed. To create an index click on the Indexed field property and then click on the button with the arrow that appears to the right-hand side. To create a unique index, choose Yes (No Duplicates) from the drop down list. To create a non-unique index, choose Yes (Duplicates OK).

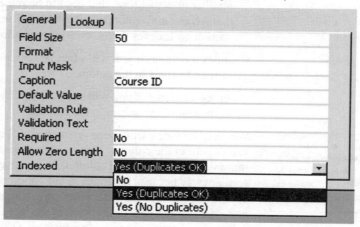

Fig 16.1
Using the Indexed property in Table design view

Creating a concatenated index

You can create indexes that are composed of more than one column in the table. These indexes are called concatenated indexes. If you will often be searching for rows using criteria specified on two or more columns, you may be able to improve performance by creating a concatenated index on those columns.

For example, if you often have to search an orders table for orders placed by a certain customer in a specified date range, a concatenated index created on the CustomerNo and OrderDate field may improve the performance of these searches.

With a concatenated index the order of the columns in the index may be important. Generally speaking, you should make the column that is most selective (that is, the one that has the fewest number of duplicate values in it) the first column in the index. If the first column in the index has many duplicate values, Access may end up doing a full table scan anyway.

To create a multiple field index, click on the View menu and then choose Indexes (or click on the Indexes button on the Table design toolbar).

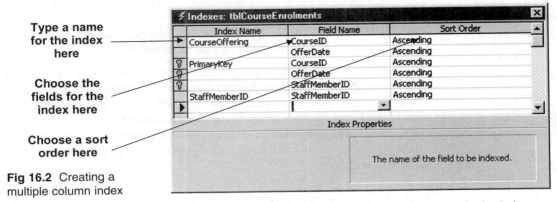

Type a name for the index here

Choose the fields for the index here

Choose a sort order here

Fig 16.2 Creating a multiple column index

In a multiple field index, the index name appears only once in the Index name column, but more than one field name appears in the field name column in the rows under the index name.

Please note, creating concatenated indexes is not so important in Access as it is in other database products. Provided that both fields have an index defined on them, Access may be able to quickly search for values by merging the two individual indexes and therefore not require a concatenated index.

Indexes that Access creates automatically

If you define a Foreign key field in a table using the Lookup wizard, Access will automatically create an index on that field. Given that the wizard is there to automate the entire process of creating Foreign keys and relationships, this is understandable. More surprising, though, is the fact that if you create a field in a table by typing a name that ends in ID and choose a data type of Number and a size of Long Integer, Access will also automatically create an index on the field.

Compacting and repairing the database

Database Management Systems that run on mainframe or mini-computers require a database administrator to look after the database to ensure its availability and smooth running. Such systems require that sufficient space for the database files is allocated on the physical devices at the time that the database is created. They may also require logical areas to be defined in these files to hold the tables and indexes. In such systems, physical storage allocation forms part of the statements that actually create the tables.

Microsoft Access, on the other hand, has been designed with minimal maintenance in mind. When you create an Access database you create the file that holds the objects in the database. As your database grows, so does the file. Unfortunately, if you delete objects of data from the database, Access does not reduce the size of the file. Worse still, if the physical disk

The size of an Access database can increase extremely quickly. You must compact the database to recover the space occupied by deleted objects or records.

on which the database file resides is fragmented, then the database file may end up spread over several sectors on the disk. This can lead to poor performance as the number of times the disk must be accessed in order to read the database file is increased by this fragmentation.

Access provides two utilities for maintaining the database file, Repair and Compact. It is recommended that you repair the database, then compact it, and then repair the compacted database. It is also good practice to make a back-up of your database before compacting or repairing it. However, if you feel that the disk that holds the database file is fragmented, you should run a Windows program such as Defrag to defragment the disk first before using the Access utilities.

Repairing the database

To repair a database follow these steps.

1. Click on the Tools menu. Choose the Database Utilities option on the menu. A sub-menu will appear. Now choose Repair database from the sub-menu.

2. If you already have a database open, Access will close the database and then start to repair it. If you do not have the database open, a File Open dialogue box will appear to enable you to select the database to repair. Select the required database file and then click on the Repair button.

3. When the repair is successfully completed, Access will display a message to that effect. In the unlikely event that Access is unable to repair the database, you may have to restore a backup copy of the database to continue working.

4. If you repaired a database that was already open, Access will now reopen the database.

Compacting the database

Access 97 will allow you to compact a database that you currently have open. However, this is not recommended. It is better to compact a closed database into a completely new file. That way, if there are any problems during the compact, you can revert to the previous (uncompacted) version of the database. To compact a database, follow these steps.

1. Close any database that you may have open.

2. Click on the Tools menu. Choose the Database Utilities option on the menu. A sub-menu will appear. Now choose Compact database from the sub-menu.

3. A File Open dialogue box will appear to enable you to select the database to compact. Select the required database file and then click on the Compact button.

4. A second dialogue box will now appear to enable you to specify the name and location of the new file that will be created by the compact operation. Type the name of the new file in the File Name box and then click on the Save button.

5. If you do not see any messages and all disk activity ceases, you know the compact operation has completed successfully (no news is good news!).

It is not a good idea to compact a database that is on a drive of a file server on a network. Copy the file to a local disk, compact into a new file on the local disk and then copy the new file back to the file server.

Other optimisation techniques

Diagnosing the cause of poor performance in a database application can be a problem, particularly if the database is held on a file server on a network. These days, PCs contain extremely fast processors and large amounts of memory. It is often the case now that the network is the slowest part of any system. If you are suffering poor performance in a database application, you may find the following tips useful.

- **Run the application on the best hardware available.** As with most Windows applications, insufficient memory can lead to performance problems from an Access database. Access needs at least 16 megabytes of memory, but the more the better. In general, increasing the memory in the PC will improve performance more than installing a faster processor.

- **Retrieve the smallest number of columns in a query.** It is tempting to create a single query that can be used for many reports. This type of query tends to include almost every field from every table that is part of the query. Although this can make maintenance easier, you may find that the query performs poorly. A query that only includes the fields that are required for the report in question may perform better.

- **Minimise the use of calculated fields in queries.** Complex calculations will slow a query down. Performing the calculation in a form or report based on the query may improve performance.

- **In multi-table queries, specify criteria on join columns in the table on the one side wherever possible.** If you need to specify criteria against a field on which a join is performed, doing so against the field on the one side of the join may mean a better performance.

- **Avoid outer joins wherever possible.** Outer joins require a full table scan on the table for which all rows are returned, and are therefore slow.

Revision exercises

1. How can an index help to improve performance in a database?

2. Which fields in a table would you normally index?

3. Which Windows utility should you run before compacting a database on a local hard drive?

4. In a multi-table query you are required to filter records on a column that implements the relationship between two tables. Should you specify the criteria on the Primary key column or the Foreign key column?

17 Social issues of information processing

What you will learn in this unit

This unit describes the social and legal issues that affect the design and implementation of information systems. At the end of this unit you should:

❒ understand that there are dangers in the use of computer systems to store and process personal information

❒ understand how the Data Protection Act was created to address some of these issues

❒ understand how that Data Protection Act can affect the work of the database designer

❒ understand why security is an important consideration when implementing information systems

❒ understand the various types of security that can be used to protect an information system

❒ describe the organisational problems that can occur as the result of the introduction of a new information system

❒ understand how health and safety issues can affect the design and implementation of information systems.

Processing personal information

Organisations have stored information about individuals as long as our society has existed. There have always been concerns about the ways that such information is gathered and the way that it is used. However, the increasing use of computers to store and process this information has lead to renewed examination of issues such as security, privacy and data protection.

There are dangers inherent in the use of computers to process information that do not arise with manual record-keeping systems. Computer systems have an almost limitless potential to store, collate and access data. As computers are networked together using public data networks, the possibility of unauthorised access is increased. It is extremely difficult, though not impossible, to remove or copy large sections of a manual record-keeping system. By contrast there is relatively little effort involved in copying data from a computer system onto removable media such as tape or magnetic disk.

Of equal concern, the potential for computers to transfer, collate and cross-refer data from differing sources has no match in manual systems. We are required to divulge personal information to a number of organisations and would be justifiably concerned if such information were to find its way into the public domain. Such privacy issues have not only led to concern from individuals and groups, but also, in many countries, to legislation being passed.

The Data Protection Act

The Data Protection Act was passed by the United Kingdom parliament in 1984. The main driving force was not public pressure for privacy legislation, but the need to conform to European standards on databases and data flows. The government of the day feared that failure to comply with EEC guidelines such as the Council of Europe's Convention for the Protection of Individuals with regard to Automatic Processing of Personal Data would prevent trade between the UK and other Member States.

The Act requires that organisations that hold personal data register with the Office of the Data Protection Registrar. The organisation should register all the categories of personal data held and the uses to which it is put.

The Act lays down eight principles regarding the correct use of personal data held on a computer. These are not a code of conduct, they have the force of law.

1. **The information to be contained in personal data shall be obtained, and personal data shall be processed, fairly and lawfully.**

    Provided that data has not been obtained by illegal means, this principle is met simply by ensuring that an organisation has appropriate registration under the Act. The Act does not seek to outlaw the use of certain types of data (such as mailing lists for junk mail), nor does it seek to limit its use, provided that the organisation is registered for that use.

2. **Personal data shall be held only for one or more specified and lawful purposes.**

    Again, this means that data can only be held for a purpose for which the organisation is registered.

3. **Personal data held for any purpose or purposes shall not be used or disclosed in any manner incompatible with that purpose, or those purposes.**

This principle basically repeats principle 2 but from the opposite point of view.

4. **Personal data held for any purpose or purposes shall be adequate, relevant and not excessive in relation to that purpose or those purposes.**

Potentially this could be used to stop the tendency for organisations to accumulate more and more data about individuals. However, the Act does not give a less woolly definition for the terms adequate, relevant and not excessive and could therefore be interpreted in a number of ways.

5. **Personal data shall be accurate and, where necessary, kept up to date.**

This is a more stringent requirement. If an organisation could be shown to have made no attempt to keep its records accurate and up to date, and if an individual could show that they had suffered loss as a result, they may be able to obtain compensation.

6. **Personal data held for any purpose or purposes shall not be kept for longer than is necessary for that purpose or those purposes.**

Again the phrase 'longer than is necessary' is open to interpretation. Much data on computer systems is subject to audit requirements that necessitate it to be held for a considerable number of years.

7. **An individual shall be entitled:**

    (a) **at reasonable intervals and without undue delay or expense -**

        (i) **to be informed by any data user whether he or she holds personal data of which the individual is the subject; and**

        (ii) **to access any such data held by a data user; and**

    (b) **where appropriate to have such data corrected or erased.**

This is possibly the key principle, since it establishes the right of an individual to know what information an organisation holds about him or her. This is often referred to as 'the Right of Subject Access'. However, there are a number of problems involved.

- Many organisations are exempt from the requirements of the Act (see below).

- An individual must make a separate enquiry for each registration that the company has made with the Registrar and pay a separate fee. This fee was set by the government of the day at £10. Some organisations have multiple registrations and checking what data they hold can be prohibitively expensive.

- If an individual has suffered loss because of inaccurate data held on a computer system, it can be extremely difficult to know whose system it was that supplied the data. For example, if you were refused credit because of inaccurate data on a credit ratings agency computer, how would you find out which agency supplied the data?

As a result of these problems, requests for subject access under this principle have been far fewer than was anticipated at the time that the Act came into force.

If an individual finds that an organisation holds inaccurate data he or she has the right to have that data corrected or erased. If necessary, the individual can apply to a court to order this correction or erasure. In addition, an individual has the right to compensation if he or she has suffered loss or damage as a result of inaccurate data being held about him or her. He or she may also be entitled to claim compensation if personal data is lost or disclosed to unauthorised persons or organisations.

8. **Appropriate security measures shall be taken against unauthorised access to, or alteration, disclosure or destruction of, personal data and against accidental loss or destruction of personal data.**

This principle speaks for itself. Again the Act does not contain a more specific definition for the term 'appropriate security'.

Exemptions to the Act

There are a number of qualifications to the principles including the following.

- **Currently the Act only applies to computerised records.** Many organisations that wish to avoid having to declare contentious information about individuals may hold that particular information on paper. You may find it surprising that, at present, this exemption extends to word processing documents.

- **Records about crime and taxation are excluded.**

- **Records associated with National Security are excluded.** This effectively means that there is no subject access to the majority of computer systems used by the government, or its agencies. The Data Protection Act can in no way be considered to provide freedom of information to citizens in the United Kingdom

- **Records associated with payroll and accounts are excluded.** However, the definition of these systems is quite limited and most human resources systems would not fall within the definition.

- **Records of a purely domestic, or other similar nature, are excluded.** This includes mailing lists used for domestic purposes, or membership records of small, unincorporated clubs.

- **Records about the dead are excluded.**

- **Records that state intentions, as opposed to facts or opinions, are excluded.** This is an odd exemption, but is mainly of academic interest.

- **Medical or social work records are excluded.** The rationale here is that such records require interpretation by an expert and therefore should not be made available.

- **Statistical or research data, or examination marks are excluded.**

How the Act affects the database designer

If you are designing a system for domestic use, the quick answer to this question is, it doesn't. However, if you are building a system that will contain personal data for an organisation that is (or should be) registered under the Act, you may need to bear some things in mind.

Your design should not allow for the inclusion of unnecessary personal data.

There is a tendency among system designers to take a 'just in case' approach to the design of systems. It is easier to make provision for all sorts of data when a system is initially designed than it is to add new fields after a system has been put into service. However, doing so may lead to problems under the Act if it could be argued that the data was excessive or irrelevant to the purpose for which it had been obtained. End users of a system can also put pressure on you to include fields in the design that are not strictly speaking necessary to the system at hand.

The Act also requires that appropriate security measures be taken to safeguard personal data. Even if you are not storing personal data, you should be concerned with security.

Security

Methods of data security have two main objectives: the prevention of deliberate or inadvertent access to data by unauthorised persons and the prevention of deliberate or inadvertent damage to data. The most important of these methods is the physical protection of computer equipment and procedural controls over its use.

The aim of computer security is to use procedures that are tough enough to prevent unauthorised access to systems, but not so arduous that they prevent genuine users of the system from effectively doing their job.

Restricting physical access to the computer system

One of the most obvious ways of improving security is to restrict physical access to the computer itself. Larger computers require special environments in which to operate reliably and it has always been the case that access to the computer room was restricted to authorised personnel. In contrast, most PCs are located in a general office environment.

Restricting physical access to a PC is an effective security method.

If you have a computer that contains sensitive or confidential information, you should make every effort to have it located in a room that can be locked and ensure that the room is locked when the system is not being used by authorised personnel. If there is a possibility that data could be lost if the machine itself were stolen, you may be able to physically secure the machine to a table or desk.

If you are worried about the disk itself being stolen, it may be possible to obtain a system that includes a lock on the system box. Alternatively, some machines have removable hard disks that can be stored in a secure location.

Restricting use of the computer system

Most systems for restricting access to systems involve the use of passwords. A PC may require a password to be entered when switched on and most modern screen savers can be password protected to ensure that an unattended system cannot be used.

If passwords are used, make sure that the passwords are not the defaults used by the manufacturer. Passwords should be changed regularly and the system should ensure that the same password is not used repeatedly.

Microsoft Access provides two levels of security for a database. The simplest method is to password protect the database file. To do this, follow these steps.

1. Close the database if it is already open.

2. Click on the File menu and then click on Open Database.

3. Select the Exclusive check box and then choose OK to open the database.

4. Click on the Tools menu, click on Security and then click on Set Database Password on the sub-menu.

5. In the Password box, type the required password. Note that passwords are case-sensitive.

6. In the Verify box, type the same password again and then click OK.

Access will require that this password be entered every time the database is opened.

Access also provides the ability to restrict access to individual objects in the database to particular users. For example, it is possible for users in the payroll department to view and update records in a salaries table, while all other users are denied access to the table. This security system is beyond the scope of this book.

Restricting network access to the computer

You should think carefully before attaching a computer that holds sensitive or confidential data to a network. With many Local Area Networks (LANs) it is possible to gain access to the hard disk of a computer on the network, even though it may not be possible to gain physical access to the machine. Even if such access can be controlled for other users, you should consider whether you would be comfortable if the network administrator could gain access to the data on this machine.

It is probably unwise to attach a modem to any machine that contains sensitive or confidential data, or to allow access to the Internet. Although the Internet is primarily a tool for downloading data to a PC from the network, it also enables information about your system to be transferred out as well.

Ensuring that policies and procedures are known and adhered to

The greatest risks to a company's data usually come from within.

Most physical means of restricting access to computer systems can be circumvented by the truly determined. Although you may be most concerned about people outside your organisation gaining access to your data, they may not represent the biggest threat. Stories about hackers may occupy many column inches in the popular press, but the fact remains that, in a commercial environment, employees or ex-employees commit most breaches of computer security.

You should ensure that policies and procedures regarding security and unauthorised access to systems are widely known and make all concerned aware that breach of such policies will be treated as a disciplinary offence.

Organisational problems when introducing new systems

The introduction of a new computer system can lead to organisational problems.

The introduction of a new computer system inevitably leads to a change in working practices in the organisation or department into which it is introduced. Although you may not be responsible for managing this change, you should be aware of the effects of change and how these effects can be manifested in terms of people's reactions to the new system.

Technophobia

Technophobia is a jargon term for fear of technology. In most case people do not fear the technology itself. Instead they fear that they will be incapable of using the new technology. People may be afraid that they may appear incompetent or that they will make mistakes that could break the entire system.

Technophobia is more often seen in older members of the workforce. It is often based on a (usually mistaken) belief that the person is too old to learn new ways of working. Although it is accepted that the older we get, the less receptive we are to new concepts, human beings are constantly learning new things throughout their lives.

Threat to status

The introduction of a new system may lead to an increase in 'office politics'.

An individual's status in an organisation is based on many things. Some people derive status from possessing information or being the only person who is able to get at the required information. These people often fear that the introduction of a new computer system will mean that anyone can have access to the information that they currently control and that they will lose their status.

These fears are often justified. One of the reasons why new systems are introduced may be that the management understands that the organisation is too reliant on that single individual and needs to provide an alternative way of accessing the information.

Changes in work patterns

The introduction of technology often results in changes to work patterns. People often fear that they will become 'slaves to the machine' and that their work routines will be driven by the processing requirements of the system. New technology may also increase the ability of management to compare the performance of one individual to another and lead to fears of competition in the workforce. All of these can lead to increased pressure and stress.

New technology can often reduce the amount of social contact in the workplace. Where individuals may have communicated information face to face, a new system may mean that communication is made electronically using e-mail or other workflow processing methods.

Fear of redundancy

The introduction of automated systems has often led to reduction in certain parts of the workforce. If this is the case, it can lead to problems. Management may want to ensure that key personnel are retained until they are no longer required, while employees may want to start looking for alternative work as soon as possible. Arranging transfers within the organisation is one effective way of dealing with this problem.

If the introduction of a new system will not lead to redundancies, this fact should be communicated clearly and promptly. There is nothing worse than losing key personnel who have found new jobs because of a rumour of redundancies.

Ways of dealing with organisational problems

There are a number of methods that can be used to reduce the types of problem described.

- Ensure that those affected are made aware of proposed changes at the earliest opportunity and have time to come to terms with what is proposed. Sudden changes will always cause the greatest problems.

- Ensure that those affected are kept fully informed throughout the process.

- Ensure that appropriate individuals are able to participate in the process. This means that appropriate individuals should be involved in the specification and design of the system.

- Ensure that the needs of the users are accurately reflected in the design of the system.

- Ensure that all users receive relevant and timely training in the new system.

Health and safety

When you are designing new systems you should also be aware of health and safety issues. The introduction of new technology may bring with it health risks. In the 1980s and 1990s there have been an increasing number of cases of Repetitive Strain Injury (or Upper Limb Disorder as it is now known) and backache reported by users of computer terminals. In some cases these problems may be more related to the psychological problems described above. In other cases they may be caused by the physical arrangement of the computer equipment or the user's position in relation to the equipment.

A badly designed system can lead to problems of stress and frustration.

As the designer of a database system, this is something over which you may have little control. However, you can increase the usability of the system that you are creating by making yourself aware of the guidelines for human factors design. Just as ergonomically designed equipment can reduce the incidence of physical ailments in knowledge workers, an ergonomically designed system can lead to less stress and pressure.

Complete texts have been written about the design of user interfaces. This section can only provide a few brief guidelines on ways to make your systems more 'user friendly'.

- **Stick to the rules**. When using a product such as Microsoft Access, you have a head start in the design of your interface because the tools that you have at your disposal are designed to comply with the interface design rules of Microsoft Windows itself. You should ensure that your system complies with the interface standards for the environment on which it is based.

- **Ensure that forms and dialogue boxes are logically laid out**. Most users will expect forms to be laid out from left to right, or from top to bottom. Avoid creating forms where pressing the Tab key results in the cursor jumping about all over the form.

- **Ensure that form designs match paper input forms.** If the user is required to transcribe data from a paper form, your screen designs should match the logical layout of the paper form as far as is practicable.

- **Ensure that the sequencing of forms matches the workflow.** If the workflow occurs in a particular sequence, your forms should also follow that sequence.

- **Use neutral colour schemes.** Tools like Microsoft Access provide you with the ability to use multiple colours on different parts of the form. You can also use bright colours on your forms. Although these may look striking or attractive to a casual user, they can lead to eye strain with continual use.

- **Don't overcrowd your forms.** Often there is a requirement to fit as much data as possible onto a single form. You may be tempted to squeeze more and more controls onto the form, or to reduce the font size used in the controls on the form. This often leads to forms that are overcrowded, confusing and difficult to read. If this happens you should consider techniques such as creating multi-page forms, or using the Tab control to create multi-page forms.

- **Ensure consistency across your form and dialogue designs.** Consistency is one of the keys to making a system user friendly. If similar forms work in different ways it can lead to frustration and poor performance. Ensure that all forms that are logically similar work in the same way.

- **Don't make the user memorise things**. The need to remember long codes or complicated commands can lead to poor performance. Offer pick lists (list boxes, combo boxes, etc) whenever possible and provide an obvious way to the features offered by the application.

- **Provide shortcuts for experienced users.** The performance of experienced users may be adversely affected if they have to use the same techniques as novice users (for example, if functions are provided only via the mouse or with menu commands). These users appreciate being able to access commonly used features using the keyboard.

- **Provide informative feedback.** If the user makes a mistake, you should ensure that the error message that the user receives is non-judgemental, explains the problem and offers a solution. However, this is not always possible. The error messages that Access generates are often extremely technical.

- **Try to prevent errors rather than handling them.** Even if your error messages are user friendly, the user will appreciate it more if you prevent the error occurring in the first place.

- **Ensure acceptance testing.** Before releasing a system to the users, it is important to ensure that they have the opportunity to test it beforehand. This is often a problem because, even if you provide the means for the users to gain access to the system, the pressure of their own jobs may mean that they do not have sufficient time to undertake adequate testing.

Revision exercises

1. Discuss the ways in which the Data Protection Act could be improved to provide a better safeguard for individuals against the misuse of personal data.

2. In what circumstances might an employee in an organisation want to misuse data that was available to him or her?

3. What techniques can be used when designing a form in an Access database to enhance its ease of use?

Appendix A Using expressions

What is an expression?

If you have used a spreadsheet product such as Microsoft Excel, you will be familiar with expressions. A formula in Excel consists of an equals sign (=) followed by an expression. An expression is anything that can be evaluated by the computer to produce a value.

The simplest example of an expression is a literal value. For example, the number 3 is an expression that can be evaluated to produce the value 3. When you enter the number 3 in the Default value property for a field in a table design, you are actually entering an expression.

More complicated expressions can be used to perform calculations. For example, $1 + 1$ is an expression that can be evaluated to produce a result of 2. Expressions are not limited to using literal values like this. An expression can refer to fields in a table or controls on a form. For example, you can create a calculated column in a query by referring to fields that exist in the table on which the query is based. In evaluating an expression such as QuantityOrdered * UnitPrice, Access will first retrieve the values in the current row for the fields referenced, then perform the mathematical calculation. The expression is therefore evaluated for each row that is returned by the query.

Where can you use expressions?

Expressions can be used to set the value of properties for most Access objects. For example, you can use an expression to specify the validation rule for a field in a table or to set the Book Color property for a text box on a form. Expressions are used to specify criteria in queries or to create calculated values in queries, forms or reports. Expressions are also the building blocks used to create programs in Visual Basic for Applications, the programming language that is built into Microsoft Access.

Types of expression

There are three fundamental types of expression, determined by the type of value that is returned when the expression is evaluated.

1. **Arithmetic expressions.** The result of an arithmetic expression is a number.

2. **Logical (or Boolean) expressions.** The result of a logical expression is only ever True, False or Null.

3. **Text (or string) expressions.** The result of a text expression is a string of characters (that is, text).

Arithmetic expressions

An arithmetic expression can be evaluated to produce a number as its result. An arithmetic expression can be a literal numeric value, but more often involves the use of an arithmetic operator in the expression. The following table shows a complete list of the arithmetic operators available in Access.

Operator	Operation	Example	Result
+	Addition	1+1	2
–	Subtraction	5–2	3
*	Multiplication	2*3	6
^	Exponentiation	3^3	27
/	Floating-point division (the result will include a decimal value)	5/2	2.5
\	Integer division (the result will only include whole numbers)	5\2	2
Mod	Modulus (remainder)	5 Mod 2	1

Access evaluates arithmetic expressions in a predetermined order. Generally expressions are evaluated from left to right, so the expression 2+4+6 gives a result of 12. However, some operators have a higher precedence than others. For example, Access will always perform multiplication before addition, so the expression 2+4*6 gives a result of 26. If you want Access to perform the arithmetic in a different order, you must enclose the part of the expression that you want to be evaluated first in brackets. For example the expression (2+4)*6 gives the result 36.

The next table shows the order of precedence for arithmetic operators.

Operator	Operation
^	Exponentiation
* /	Multiplication, floating-point division
\	Integer division
Mod	Modulus
+ −	Addition, subtraction

Arithmetic expressions involving Nulls

You should be aware that any arithmetic expression involving a Null value will evaluate to Null. This is because a Null represents an unknown value. When you think about it, this makes sense. The result of multiplying an unknown value by two can only be another unknown value.

Logical expressions

Logical expressions compare two or more values to produce either True, False or Null. For example, the expression 1=1 gives a value of True, whereas the expression 1=2 gives the value False. The values True and False are often referred to as Boolean values after the name of the English mathematician George Boole who developed the form of logic that uses two values. However, since any logical expression containing a Null will evaluate to Null, databases such as Access use a three valued logic, which can make life more complicated than you might wish.

Logical expressions are frequently used as criteria for queries to restrict the rows that are returned. Access provides a number of operators for performing comparisons in logical expressions.

Comparison operators

Operator	Means	Example	Result
=	Equal to (Access will usually omit the equals sign when specifying criteria in a query)	1=1	True
<	Less than specified value	2<5	True
>	Greater than specified value	2>5	False
<>	Not equal to specified value	2<>5	True
<=	Less than or equal to specified value	3<=3	True
>=	Greater than or equal to specified value	3>=4	False
Between ... And ...	Between two specified values	Between 2 And 5	True

If any of the values involved in the comparison are Null, the result of the expression will also be Null.

Text comparison operators

Text comparison operators are provided in the table below.

Operator	Means
="value"	Matches specified value exactly (Access will usually omit the equals sign when specifying criteria in a query)
Like "value*"	Matches any string of characters beginning with value

Using the Like operator you can specify 'wild card' characters to make partial matches of values. You can use the following wild card characters with the Like operator.

Wild card character	Does
?	Matches values that have any single character in the same position as the question mark. For example, "Sm?th" will find both Smith and Smyth, but will not match Wildsmith or Smithers
*	Matches any number of characters in the same position as the asterisk. For example, "*guay" would find Paraguay and Uruguay

Other logical operators

The following operators will also return a Boolean value.

Operator	Means	Example	Result
Not	Negates an expression	Not True	False
And	Logical And	1=1 And 2=2	True
Or	Logical Or	1=1 Or 3=2	True
In (value list)	Matches any value in value list (can only be used in queries)	3 In(2,3,4)	True
Is Null	Compares value to Null (can only be used in queries, elsewhere use IsNull() function)	IsNull(3)	False

Is Null provides the only way to determine whether a value is Null. If you compare a Null with any other value, the result will be Null – even if the other value is Null!

Remember the following points.

- A Null is never equal to (=) any other value, including another Null.

- A Null is never Not equal to (<>) any other value.

- A Null is never less than or greater than any other value.

String expressions

Access also provides two operators for working with string expressions.

Operator	Operation	Example	Result
+	Concatenates (joins together) two strings	"Fred" + "Bloggs"	"Fred Bloggs"
&	Concatenates (joins together) two strings	"Fred" & "Bloggs"	"Fred Bloggs"

The difference between the two string operators is how each copes with Null values. If you use the + operator, the expression will evaluate to Null if any of the values in the expression are Null. In contrast, the & operator treats individual Null values as zero length strings (blank text). The & operator will only return Null if all values in the expression are Null.

Functions

Access provides a number of functions that can be used in expressions. Functions in Access work like the functions that you use in formulas in a spreadsheet such as Excel. You pass values to the function for it to use. These values are called arguments. The arguments have to be of the correct data type and the correct order, otherwise an error will occur. The function in turn returns a value.

Bear in mind that you are not limited to using literal values in functions. In the same way that you can pass the address of a range to a function in Excel, you can pass the name of a field as an argument to a function in Excel. Access will first attempt to evaluate the value in the field before evaluating the result of the function.

Functions can be grouped according to their use. What follows is a selection of the most commonly used functions. The Access help system contains a full reference to all built-in functions.

Date functions

Access provides a range of functions for working with dates and intervals. For a discussion of the ways that dates and intervals can be manipulated, see Unit 7 on Data design.

Function	Use	Example	Result
Now()	Returns the current system date and time	=Now()	The current date and time
Date()	Returns the current system date	=Date()	The current date
DateAdd()	Returns a date to which a specified date interval has been added	=DateAdd("m", -1, #31-Aug-96#)	31/07/96
DateDiff()	Returns the number of time intervals between two dates	=DateDiff("m", #1/1/96#, #31/8/96#)	7
DatePart()	Returns specified part of date	=DatePart("w", #25-Dec-96#)	4 (Wednesday)

Mathematical functions

Function	Use	Example	Result
Abs()	Returns the absolute value of a number	=Abs(-1)	1
Sqr()	Returns the square root of a number	=Sqr(9)	3
Log()	Returns the logarithm of a number	=Log(9)	2.197225

Financial functions

Function	Use	Example	Result
SLN()	Returns the straight line depreciation of an asset for a given period	=SLN(100, 20, 5)	16
PV()	Returns the present value of an investment	=PV(.0825, 20, -5000, 1000000, 1)	50117.9

String manipulation functions

Function	Use	Example	Result
Trim()	Trims leading and trailing spaces from a string	=Trim(" Joe ")	"Joe"
Left()	Returns the leftmost *n* characters of string	=Left("Microsoft", 5)	"Micro"
Right()	Returns the rightmost *n* characters of string	=Right("Microsoft", 5)	"osoft"
Mid()	Returns characters from the middle of a string	=Mid("Microsoft", 5, 2)	"os"

Lookup and aggregate functions

Function	Use	Example	Result
DLookup()	Looks up a value matching criteria in a domain	=DLookup("[LastName]", "tblStaffMembers", "[EmployeeNo] = 256")	"Perigault"
DCount()	Counts values matching criteria in a domain	= DCount("*", " tblStaffMembers ", "[Trainer] = True")	4

Access also provides Dsum, DMax, Dmin, DFirst, Dlast, Dvar and DstdDev functions. These aggregate functions work like the aggregate functions in a Totals query, but they can be used outside of a query. For example, an expression using one of these functions can be used to set the ControlSource property of an unbound text box on a form.

You can also use the following functions to calculate group values on a form or report.

Function	Use	Example	Result
SUM()	Returns the sum of the values in a field	=SUM([Cost])	The sum of purchase prices in the group
AVG()	Returns the average (mean) of the values in a field	=AVG([Cost])	The average purchase price in the group
COUNT()	Returns the number of values in a field	=COUNT([EmployeeNo])	The number of employees in the group
MIN()	Returns the minimum value in a field	=MIN([Cost])	The lowest purchase price in the group
MAX()	Returns the maximum value in a field	=MAX([Cost])	The highest purchase price in the group

Logical functions

Function	Use	Example	Result
IIf()	Returns one of two arguments depending on the evaluation of an expression	= IIf(Date()=#01/01/96#, "Happy new year", "Just another day")	"Just another day" unless it is new year's day 1996 when it returns "Happy new year"

Using the expression builder

The expression builder is a tool that is provided with Microsoft Access to assist in the creation of expressions. Instead of having to remember all the details needed to construct an expression, the builder allows you to pick from available options.

When you select a property in the Properties window for an object in an Access database, you will often see a button appear with an elipsis (...) on it. If you click on this button, a builder or wizard will be started to help you set the value of the property. In cases where the property expects a source of data to be specified, clicking on this button will display the Query design window. In cases where an expression can be specified, clicking on this button will display the Expression Builder.

The Expression Builder has several sections as shown in figure A.1.

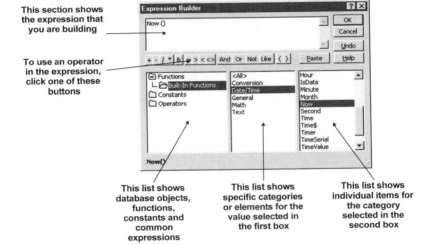

This section shows the expression that you are building

To use an operator in the expression, click one of these buttons

This list shows database objects, functions, constants and common expressions

This list shows specific categories or elements for the value selected in the first box

This list shows individual items for the category selected in the second box

Fig A.1
Constructing an expression using the Expression Builder

To create an expression using the Expression Builder, follow these steps.

1. In the list in the bottom left of the Expression Builder, choose the type of object or element you want to work with. For example, to create an expression using a built-in function, double-click on the Functions folder and then choose Built-In Functions. The list in the bottom centre of the builder will display a list of categories of built-in functions.

2. In the list in the bottom centre, double-click on an element or click on a category of elements. For example, to create an expression using a date function, click on the Date/Time category. The list on the bottom right will display a list of the functions in the chosen category.

3. In the list in the bottom right, double-click on the element required to copy it into the box at the top of the Expression Builder. For example, to use the Now function, double-click on Now in the list in the bottom right.

4. To build a more complicated expression, repeat the above steps. To include arithmetic, comparison or other operators in the expression, use the appropriate button in the middle of the Expression Builder window.

5. When you have finished building the expression, click on the OK button. The expression in the top part of the builder will be pasted into the Property from which the builder was started.

Appendix B
Evaluating Microsoft Access against Codd's 12 rules for a relational database

In 1985 Dr E F Codd, the originator of the relational model for database management, published a paper called 'Is your database really relational?' In this paper he set down a number of rules (referred to as Codd's 12 rules, although there are actually 13 of them – Rule 0 serves as a foundation on which all the others are based) with which a system must comply to be considered fully relational.

The paper came about because of an increasing trend in the early 1980s for database vendors to describe their existing products as relational, or as being 'based on the relational model'. At that time the term 'relational' was the computing industry's hot buzzword (much as 'object-oriented' is the key buzzword for the 1990s).

Since the paper was published the rules have been used to evaluate database management systems that are claimed to be relational. This section explains each rule in turn and evaluates whether Access complies with the rule.

Rule 0. For any system that is advertised as, or claims to be, a relational database management system, that system must be able to manage databases entirely through its relational capabilities.

The main purpose of this rule is to ensure that a product does not require or advise its users to revert to any non-relational capabilities for the management of data. At the time that the paper was written many vendors were claiming that their products were relational when, in fact, they were based on the hierarchical or network model with some kind of relational preprocessing capability.

Although the vendor would advertise the product as being relational, the technical documentation for the product would often advise users to implement the database using the features supplied by the older model. These database models maintain relationships between tables by the use of physical mechanisms such as record pointers, rather than by the use of the data values held in Foreign keys. The usual reason given for this advice was 'to achieve acceptable performance'.

Since Access was designed from the outset as a relational database it is able to manage databases entirely through its relational capabilities. Access complies fully with Rule 0.

Rule 1. All information in a relational database is represented at the logical level in exactly one way – by values in tables.

There are several points raised by this rule. Firstly that data is represented at a logical level that is distinct from the physical storage method that is used. At the logical level tables that are an arrangement of rows and columns represent all data. These tables have two important characteristics.

a. The order of the columns is not important. If you rearrange the columns, the meaning of the data will not be changed in any way.

b. The ordering of the rows is not important. If you rearrange the rows, the meaning of data in the individual rows will not be changed.

Access tables behave in just this way. In fact, in Access the order of the rows in a table cannot be guaranteed unless they have been explicitly sorted. This fact, together with the lack of record numbers in Access, is a cause of particular difficulty to dBASE, FoxPro and Clipper programmers moving to the product.

Microsoft Access complies fully with Rule 1.

Rule 2. Each and every datum (atomic value) in a relational database is guaranteed to be logically accessible by resorting to a combination of a table name, Primary key value and column name.

The point of this rule is that, given the data value of a Primary key, it is possible to retrieve all the other column values for the row that are uniquely identified by that Primary key value. In many non-relational systems it is only possible to retrieve certain records by identifying the physical address of the location where the record is stored (by means of a record pointer). To be considered relational, the database must preserve the independence of the logical view of the data from the physical access methods used to retrieve it.

Microsoft Access complies fully with Rule 2.

Rule 3. Null values (distinct from the empty character string or a string of blank characters and distinct from zero or any other number) are supported for representing missing information and inapplicable information in a systematic way, independent of data type.

In many non-relational systems it is necessary to define a special value to represent missing information. However, each column may represent the missing data using a different value. This means that a user designing a query to retrieve records with missing information would need to know these 'false' values for each column concerned.

The main point here is that the treatment of missing values should be handled in a systematic way, rather than on a per column basis. Arguments over the appropriateness of Nulls to represent missing values have raged for many years. The use of defined values to represent missing data is discussed in Unit 7 on data design.

Although the rule states that Null values must be supported, it is accepted that certain columns will need to be defined with a constraint that disallows Null values (for example, in the Primary key).

Microsoft Access complies fully with Rule 3.

Rule 4. The database description is represented at the logical level in the same way as ordinary data, so that authorised users can apply the same relational language to its interrogation as they apply to the regular data.

In a relational database the definitions of the objects that make up the database (the tables, views and so on) are themselves held in tables. The tables that hold the data about the database (which is known as the meta-data) are often referred to as the system tables or the system catalogue. It should be possible to view the data held in the system catalogue using the same techniques that are used to retrieve the regular data values.

Microsoft Access does store information about the database in a set of system tables (these tables, which are prefixed Msys, are usually hidden from view). However, it is not possible to view the data in some of these tables. This is because information that is used by the security system in Access is also stored in these tables together with other data about the database. If the user could view this data, it might be possible to subvert the security of the database.

Access provides another means to obtain information about the system catalogue using the Data Access Objects (DAO) library and the Visual Basic for Applications (VBA) programming language. However, VBA is not a relational language.

Microsoft Access does not comply fully with Rule 4.

Rule 5. A relational system must support several languages and various modes of terminal use (for example, the fill-in-the-blanks mode). However, there must be at least one language whose statements can express all of the following items:

- **data definitions**
- **view definitions**
- **data manipulation (interactive and by program)**
- **integrity constraints**

- **authorisation**

- **transaction boundaries.**

The main point of this rule is to ensure that the user of the database need only learn one language to perform the data definition and data manipulation tasks required to manage the database. In addition, Codd mentions that by using the single language it should be possible to perform these tasks without taking the database off-line.

The Structured Query Language (SQL) language provides constructs for each of these items, as explained below.

Item	Purpose	SQL statement	Access SQL support?
Data definition	The creation of table definitions within the database schema	CREATE TABLE...	Yes
View (query) definition	The creation of view definitions within the database schema	CREATE VIEW...	No, but queries can be defined using Query By Example (QBE)
Data manipulation (interactive and by program)	The retrieval and manipulation of data values, including the adding, updating and deletion of rows	SELECT.. INSERT... UPDATE... DELETE...	Yes
Integrity constraints	The definition of constraints which control data values that may be entered into tables	Sub-clauses of CREATE or ALTER table statements	Yes
Authorisation	The definition of security measures that control access to the database or to individual objects in the database	GRANT... REVOKE...	No, Access security is defined interactively using the Access interface
Transaction boundaries	The ability to define multiple updates as a single logical unit that must all be completed, or must all fail. For example, posting a debit to one account and a credit to another account must both take place to ensure the integrity of the data.	BEGIN TRANS COMMIT ROLLBACK	No, only available in Visual Basic for Application programs using Data Access Objects

Where Access does not provide a given capability using SQL, it can be achieved using the DAO library by writing programs using the VBA programming language. However, as noted previously, VBA is not a relational language.

Microsoft Access does not comply fully with Rule 5.

Rule 6. All views that are theoretically updateable are also updateable by the system.

Although a view may contain data from more than one table, in cases where it presents single identifiable data values it should be able to perform updates to those values. This includes the insertion and deletion of records in the tables concerned.

Microsoft Access complies fully with Rule 6. It is worth noting that many of the 'big name' relational database products do not support updateable views.

Rule 7. The capability of handling a base relation or a derived relation (that is, a view) as a single operand applies not only to the retrieval of data but also to the insertion, update and deletion of data.

A relational language does not make requests for data one record at a time. Instead it requests sets of data values. For example, the SQL statement SELECT * FROM Courses WHERE TrainerID = 7 may retrieve one or many rows. This rule requires that statements that insert, update or delete rows should also work on data sets, rather than on one record at a time. Thus the SQL statement DELETE * FROM Courses WHERE TrainerID = 7 may delete one or many rows.

Access supports the insertion, deletion and updating of data values in multiple rows using action queries as well as the corresponding SQL data manipulation statements (INSERT, UPDATE and DELETE).

Microsoft Access complies fully with Rule 7.

Rule 8. Applications programs and terminal activities remain logically unimpaired whenever changes are made in storage representations or access methods.

This rule states that the logical representation of the data must be completely independent of the physical methods used to store that data. In non-relational systems this is rarely the case.

Microsoft Access complies fully with Rule 8.

Rule 9. Application programs and terminal activities remain logically unimpaired when information preserving changes of any kind that theoretically permit unimpairment are made to the base tables.

The main point of this rule is that if changes are made to the database schema, it should be possible to reconstruct the previous schema by the definition of views. For example, a single table could split into two either by rows (based on Primary key values) or by putting some columns in the first table and the other columns in the second table. Provided that the Primary key values are preserved in both tables, it should be possible to define a view that would reconstruct the original table (in the first case you could define a Union query, in the second a simple join).

Codd goes on to say that it should be possible to perform updates, insertions and deletions on the newly created views. Therefore a prerequisite of compliance with this rule is compliance with Rule 6.

Microsoft Access complies fully with Rule 9.

Rule 10. Integrity constraints specific to a particular relational database must be definable in the relational data sub-language and storable in the catalogue, not in the applications programs.

This rule states that any integrity constraints defined for a database must be stored in the database itself (as part of the system catalogue) and not as part of an application that uses the database.

It is worth noting that many 'big name' database systems have only just implemented this facility. Many products required that referential integrity constraints be defined using triggers. Triggers are small programs, often written in a version of SQL that has been extended to include procedural programming constructs. Although triggers are usually stored in the database, they do not form part of the system catalogue.

Access, on the other hand, stores integrity constraints within its system tables. Referential integrity can be defined using sub-clauses of the CREATE or ALTER table SQL statements, and this information is stored in a system table called MsysRelationships. Other constraints can be defined as table properties, or using SQL data definition statements, and are stored in the catalogue tables.

Microsoft Access complies fully with Rule 10.

Rule 11. The data manipulation sub-language of a relational database management system must enable application programs and enquiries to remain logically the same whether, and whenever, data are physically centralised or distributed.

This rule states that whether the data in a database is held in a single location or distributed over multiple locations, the programming statements required to manipulate that data should be the same. Thus the location of the data is transparent to the user.

Access does well on this point. Not only is it possible to manipulate data held in multiple locations in the native Access format (using linked tables), it is also possible to manipulate data in multiple database formats as if it were native Access data. For example, using Access it is possible to join records in a native Access table on one machine, to records in a dBASE IV table on another machine, to records in a table in an Oracle database on another machine (running under a different operating system). However, the performance of such an arrangement may be less than optimal.

Note that this rule refers to the distribution of data, not to the distribution of processing that data.

Microsoft Access complies fully with Rule 11.

Rule 12. If a relational system has a low-level (single-record-at-a-time) language, that low-level language cannot be used to subvert or bypass the integrity rules and constraints expressed in the higher level relational language (multiple-records-at-a-time).

Many Database Management Systems (DBMS) products include the capability to work with data in a database one record at a time. Microsoft Access provides this facility using the DAO library that can be manipulated using the VBA programming language.

Using DAO it is possible to update values in a query in an inconsistent way. For example, when opening a record set using DAO it is possible to specify that inconsistent updates are allowable. If the record set is based on a query that joins records from two tables on a particular column, it is possible to update that column in the first table to a value that is not the same as the value in the same column in the other table. The tables would therefore be left in an inconsistent state.

Although Access will not allow updates to the record set that violate any referential integrity constraints defined in the database, using such an update it may be possible to leave the database in an inconsistent state. Such an update would not be allowed in the SQL language.

Microsoft Access does not comply fully with Rule 12.

It is worth noting that, while Access breaks this rule on something of a technicality, other products break this rule completely and deliberately. Oracle, for example, includes a utility called SQL*Loader that provides a facility to perform 'direct path loading'. Using this option it is possible to write whole database blocks directly to the database, bypassing SQL completely.

Conclusion

We have seen that Microsoft Access does not fully comply with Codd's 12 rules. However, it should be noted that many other products that could not be considered as anything other that relational do not comply with all the rules. In his original paper, Codd noted that "no existing DBMS product that I know of can honestly claim to be fully relational, at this time".

In some cases Access fails a rule because the version of SQL implemented in the product does not implement the language element required to provide support. For example, it is not possible to create views using Access SQL because it does not support the CREATE VIEW statement. It is important to note, however, that Access provides the ability to create views (queries) using the Query By Example (QBE) interface, which is much more user-friendly than using SQL statements. It is also possible to create queries programmatically using VBA and the DAO library.

At the time that his paper was published, Codd effectively stated that a score of 6 out of 12 was "good, but improvable". A reasonable score for Access would be 9½ out of 12.

Appendix C Glossary

Aggregate functions Functions that can be used to group, total and perform descriptive statistics on data. These functions can be used in a query or in SQL statements to provide summary data from the individual records. Examples of aggregate functions include SUM, COUNT, AVERAGE, MAX and MIN.

Application software Computer programs written to perform a particular task or end-user function. Examples of applications include accounting and payroll systems, Computer Aided Design, sales and order processing. An application may use the data or services provided by a database management system, but are usually not components of the database itself (although they may be stored within the database). Contrast with Systems software.

Arc In an Entity-Relationship diagram, an arc is a way of identifying two or more mutually exclusive relationships.

ASCII An encoding system for character data (stands for American Standard Code for Information Interchange). Since all data is stored inside a computer as numbers, a coding system is required to convert letters into numbers. ASCII is the system used on PCs and most mini-computers. Most mainframe systems, as well as IBM's mini-computers, use a different (and incompatible) encoding system known as EBCDIC (which stands for Extended Binary Coded Decimal Interchange Code). The character set used can affect the order in which rows are sorted in a query.

Attribute In an Entity-Relationship diagram, an attribute is a single data item that can be used to identify, classify, quantify, qualify or describe the state of an entity. In the relational database model, attribute is the technical term used to describe a column in a table.

Auditing The process of examining the records kept by an organisation to verify their correctness. Since so many records are now kept in databases, there may be a requirement to store additional data in the database whose sole purpose is to enable the auditing process.

Authentication A security procedure in which a user of a system is asked to identify themselves using a token (such as a password) that should only be known by them. This process is often called 'logging on'.

Back-up The process of copying the files (or images of the files) onto removable media such as floppy disks or magnetic tape. The back-up represents a consistent image of the database at a particular time. If the database suffers a system crash, such as a disk drive becoming unusable, it is possible to restore the database to its state at the time the back-up was made. Only changes made since the back-up was made may be lost. In larger systems even these changes may not be lost, since a separate record of each transaction may be written to a transaction or roll back log. These logs can be reapplied to the database to perform a complete recovery.

Batch processing An arrangement where transactions are processed in groups known as batches. In the past, transactions were collected throughout the day and then processed in a batch, usually overnight. These days, transactions are mainly processed on-line, but reconciliation and extraction processes may still be performed in batch mode.

Business rule An organisational rule that governs the storage or processing of data. Business rules may be implemented as constraints in a database, as processing logic in an application program, or as manual procedures, policies or working practices.

Calculated column A column in a query or view that is derived by calculations performed on values in other columns. The calculation is performed for each row that is returned by the query.

Candidate key It is possible that two different columns could be used to uniquely identify the rows in a table. These columns are known as candidate keys. The database designer must decide which of the columns to use as the Primary key. The one that is rejected is called an Alternate key.

Cardinality The minimum and maximum number of occurrences of the entities that can partake in a relationship. In the majority of cases, relationships have a cardinality of 'one-to-many'.

Cartesian product A relational database operation that returns all possible combination of rows from each of the tables in a view. This is what you get if you do not specify a join between two tables in a query. If each table contains 500 rows, the resulting view will return 250,000 rows (usually after a long wait).

Cascading delete A rule enforced by the database that ensures that if a row is deleted in one table, all related rows in other tables will also be deleted.

Cascading update A rule enforced by the database that ensures that if the Primary key for a row in one table is updated, all foreign key values in related rows in other tables will also be updated. Some purists would argue that it should not be possible to update Primary Key values, but Access offers this facility.

Catalogue A term used to describe the system tables in a database – that is, the tables used by the database itself to store information about the objects contained in the database. These tables are often hidden from users of the database.

Client-server A processing mode in which the processing is undertaken by two or more independent software components communicating with each other. The term client-server is often used to describe a system in which the software for displaying the user interface and much of the application processing is executed on an individual's workstation (often a Windows-based PC). The processing that is undertaken to store and manipulate data is executed on a separate computer (called a server). These two separate computers communicate with each other over a network.

Collating sequence The way in which the characters in a computer's set of printable characters are ordered. This affects the way that text values are ordered when they are sorted.

Column In the relational model each column implements an attribute in a data model. A column holds information about a single data item.

Composite key A key that consists of two or more columns in a table. Also called a concatenated key. A composite key may be required when the value in a single column is not sufficient to uniquely identify a row in a table, but the combination of two values is guaranteed to be unique.

Computer Aided Systems Engineering (CASE) Computer-based tools for producing graphical models of systems, documenting requirements or assisting the design and creation of systems. Some CASE products may also include tools for the automatic generation of database objects or application programs.

Conceptual data model A model of the data storage requirements of an organisation which is represented in a way that is independent of any physical means of storing the data. An Entity-Relationship diagram (if drawn correctly) is an example of a conceptual data model.

Constraint A rule that is held in the database and enforced by the database management system to ensure the integrity of data. For example, a column may have a 'not Null' constraint. As a result, the database management system will ensure that all records contain a value in that column. If they do not, the insert or update operation will be rejected.

Correlated sub-query A query nested within a query. The sub-query references values returned by the outer query, and is therefore evaluated once for each row returned by the outer query.

Data Facts or opinions regarding people, objects, places, events or anything else of significance to a person or an organisation.

Data administrator A person in an organisation who has responsibility for the information resources of an organisation. The data administrator may define or enforce standards for the naming, storage or implementing of data items to ensure consistency and integrity of the data held in the various systems used in an organisation.

Data conversion The act of converting data from one method of storage to another. Also known as data migration. The time and effort required to perform data migration is often severely underestimated in a project. If the quality of the data to be converted is poor, much effort may be required to 'clean it up' before it can be loaded into the new system.

Data Definition Language (DDL) A programming language that can be used to define the objects that make up a database. Structured Query Language (SQL) is an example of a language that includes Data Definition capabilities.

Data integrity The control of data to ensure that it is accurate, correct and relates properly with other data. Database management systems provide mechanisms to ensure the integrity of data in the database (usually by preventing invalid data from being entered in the first place).

Data item A single fact or opinion about something. The smallest named unit of data in a system.

Data Manipulation Language (DML) A programming language that can be used to retrieve and manipulate the data in a database. Structured Query Language (SQL) is an example of a language that includes Data Manipulation capabilities.

Data security The protection of computerised information by various means. These include the restriction of physical access to computer equipment, controlling access to systems by means of identification and authentication, encryption of data, as well as organisational policies and procedures.

Data type The type of data that a column or attribute may store. Examples of data types include Text, Number or Date. If a column is defined as a date, the Database Management System (DBMS) will only permit values that can be recognised as dates in that column.

Data warehouse A large database system, that incorporates data from many other databases, often in summary format. Users can analyse this data in various ways without affecting the transaction processing systems that supply the data. A data warehouse is usually designed to make this analysis as efficient as possible, whereas a transaction processing system is usually optimised for data entry.

Database An integrated collection of data organised to meet the needs of one or more users.

Database administrator A person in an organisation whose job it is to ensure that a database is implemented correctly and is available when required. Most PC database products do not require a database administrator. Larger systems may require an administrator to perform tasks such as ensuring that data files are appropriately sized for the data that they are required to hold, to perform back-ups, and so on. A database administrator may actually implement the data design passed to them by a designer.

Database Management System (DBMS) A computerised system used to structure and manipulate data. The system should also provide tools to ensure the integrity and security of the data.

Database server In a networked environment, a database server is one or more computers dedicated to running the Database Management System software The data is held on hard disks attached to this machine and the database processing is undertaken by the CPU in this machine.

Deadlock This situation occurs when one transaction cannot be completed because it is waiting for a resource that it being used by another process. The other process, in turn, is waiting for a resource that is being used by the first process. Neither process can ever be completed. Also known as a 'deadly embrace'.

Denormalisation The process of introducing intentional redundancy into tables for performance reasons. This redundant data may involve storing data that could be derived by calculation, or by merging columns from two tables into a single table to avoid having to join them in a view.

Device A piece of hardware that performs a specific function.

Difference A relational operation which selects the rows in one table that do not have related rows in another table.

Distributed database A database whose component parts are located on more than one physical computer, connected by some form of communications network. Despite being located on more than one machine, the database will appear to the user as one logical unit.

Documentation Documents, either on paper or in electronic form, that record the design and implementation for a system or describe how it works (either for use by users of the system or other developers). This is usually the first thing to go when the development schedule gets tight.

Domain A set of values that can be used to describe or constrain what can be stored in a particular data item. A domain may consist of a simple list of applicable values or a range of values described by its lower and upper bounds.

Encryption The encoding of data so that it cannot be understood without knowing how to decode it.

Entity In an Entity-Relationship diagram, an entity is any thing of significance about which information needs to be held.

Entity integrity The requirement to uniquely identify each column in a table so that it can be accessed by the database, and for each row to be uniquely identified by means of a Primary key that cannot contain a Null value. A requirement of the relational model that is not enforced by the majority of relational databases.

Entity-Relationship (ER) model A set of diagrams that represent entities and the relationships between them. The diagrams may also show the individual attributes for each entity.

Equi-join A join between two tables in a query that will return rows only when the values in the columns on which the join is made are equal (and not Null).

Executive Information System A system that supports managerial decision making rather than the day-to-day operations of an organisation. Also known as a Decision Support System. Large Executive Information Systems may form part of a Data warehouse.

Expression A set of actions that can be evaluated to produce a result. For example, the expression 1 + 1 involves performing addition on two literal numbers and can be evaluated to give a result of 2.

Field A way of identifying a single data item in a file. Some database products (Microsoft Access included) use the term field to refer to an individual column within a table.

File The physical means of storing one or more objects in a database on a mass storage device.

File server A computer on a network that is used for storing shared files. Files are held on hard disks attached to this machine but the CPU in this machine does not undertake any processing other than delivering the contents of these files to client workstations.

Filtering Selecting a sub-set of the rows in a table by comparing the values in one or more columns to a set of supplied criteria.

Foreign key One or more columns in a table that are used to implement a relationship to another table. To implement the relationship, the Primary key columns of one table are duplicated in the related table.

Format The representation of a particular value on an output medium (such as the screen or printed on paper). This representation may differ from the value that is actually stored in the database.

Functional dependence One attribute in an entity is functionally dependent on another attribute in the same entity if by knowing the value of the first attribute you can determine the value of the other. For example, if you know the name of a country you can find out the name of its capital city. The capital city attribute is functionally dependent on the country name attribute.

Hardware The physical or mechanical parts of a computer system.

Homonym The same word used to mean more than one thing in different contexts or by different parts of an organisation.

Index An index in a database works like an index in a book. To find the row, or rows, that contain a particular value, the database can search in the index to find the location of the row rather than having to search through the entire table. Indexes can be used to increase the performance of searching and sorting operations.

Information Data that has been organised in some way so as to make it useful or meaningful to someone.

Input device A piece of hardware used to input data into a computer system. Examples of input devices include the keyboard, mouse, scanner, light pen and so on.

Instance A single occurrence of an entity. Given an entity representing countries of the world, France represents a single instance of that entity type.

Integrity constraint A rule that can be enforced by a Database Management System to ensure the accuracy and applicability of data in a database.

Intersection A relational database operation which forms a virtual table (a view) that holds the rows that are common to two or more tables.

Join A relational database operation used to return columns from two or more tables. Joins can be performed on columns that share the same data type. The most common form of join (equi-join) returns rows where the values in the columns on which the join is made are the same (and not Null). However, comparison operators other than equivalence can be used to join the tables.

Key One or more columns in a table that are often used to retrieve values from a table.

Link entity An entity introduced into a Entity-Relationship diagram to resolve a many-to-many relationship between two other entities (known as cardinal entities). A link entity is also known as an associative or intersection entity.

Lock A procedure used by a database to control multiple access to individual rows in a table. To prevent a row being changed by two or more users at the same time, the database can put a lock on the record to prevent the other users from being able to edit the row. In many databases (Access included), the database will actually lock physical disk pages, which may result in more than a single row being locked at the same time.

Logical data independence A property of a Database Management System that allows the physical reorganisation of the files that make up the database, without the need to make any changes to application programs that use the data. This is in contrast to many older file processing systems in which changes to the data files could result in a need to rewrite and recompile application programs.

Mainframe A large and expensive multi-purpose computer that can be used by hundreds of users at the same time.

Many-to-many relationship A relationship between two entities in which many instances of one entity can be related to many instances of the other entity. For example, many employees may attend a training course and each employee can attend many training courses (over time). Many-to-many relationships are not permitted in an Entity-relationship model and cannot be implemented directly in a relational database.

Memory Temporary electronic storage location for data and programs that are currently being used in the system. When a computer loses power, the contents of the memory are lost.

Meta data Data that describes the structure of a data model or a database system. Meta data may be stored in a data dictionary or in a CASE tool and forms the catalogue in a Database Management System.

Non-procedural language A programming language in which the programmer states the problem to be solved, but not the steps that are required to produce the solution. Structured Query Language (SQL) is an example of a non-procedural language.

Normalisation A step-by-step process used to decompose complex data structures into simple entities.

Null A special value that a column in a table can hold to indicate that it holds no current value. This may be because the value is unknown, missing or inapplicable to the particular column.

Object Linking and Embedding (OLE) A PC standard for communication between different applications and for storing documents or components created in one application in another application.

On-Line Analytical Processing (OLAP) A type of processing in which users can perform dimensional analysis (what if scenarios) in an on-line environment. This is in contrast to traditional batch processing where users were limited to a fixed set of reports that would be produced overnight.

On-Line Transaction Processing (OLTP) A type of processing in which business transactions are processed in real time using a computer system. The results of a transaction are immediately available in the database. Older systems utilised a technique known as batch processing in which transactions were gathered over time into units of work known as a batch. Each batch was applied to the database as a single unit (often overnight).

Operator An action that can be performed on a numeric, text or logical value. For example, two numbers can be added together using the addition operator, which is represented by the + symbol in most computer software.

Optimiser Part of a Database Management System that attempts to find the most efficient way to execute a query, usually by utilising appropriate indexes on the tables concerned.

Outer join A join in a query that returns all the rows in a particular table whether or not there are related records in the table to which it is being joined.

Output device A piece of hardware used to display information from a computer system. Examples of output devices include the screen, printers, plotters, Computer Output Microfiche and so on.

Peer-to-peer network A network that is implemented without a file server. A workstation can share its local hard disk with other workstations on the network and use another workstation's hard disk if it has also been shared. Other peripheral devices such as printers can also be shared.

Physical design The process of converting a logical data model into the structures that can be used to implement the design using a manual system or a particular computerised system.

Primary key The set of columns in a table that are used to uniquely identify each row in the table. The Database Management System (DBMS) will enforce the uniqueness of the items in the column and ensure that values are supplied for all columns that make up the Primary key.

QBE (Query By Example) A method of creating a query to retrieve data from a database, originally developed by IBM in the early 1970s. Instead of defining the query by writing statements in a programming language, with QBE it is possible to indicate the columns that are required interactively using a grid, and to filter the data using example values. Microsoft considerably enhanced the technique for Access by using the Windows Graphical User Interface.

Record In a file processing system, a record is a single entry in a file. Some database products (Microsoft Access included) use the term record to refer to an individual row within a table.

Recursive relationship A relationship between an entity and itself. Often used to model hierarchies.

Referential integrity Rules in a database that ensure that data is valid and consistent. Whereas individual constraints can be used to ensure the validity of data in a single column or a table, referential integrity constraints ensure the validity of data between tables.

Referential integrity constraints are usually implemented against Foreign keys or when a relationship is defined. If a Foreign key is defined with referential integrity, the database will ensure that a row containing the same Primary key value exists in the related table.

Relation The technical term for a table in a database – a named collection of columns.

Relational Database Management System (RDBMS) A database system based on the relational model.

Relational model A database model in which data is represented as a collection of tables and relationships between them are implemented by matching data values (as opposed to physical structures).

Relationship In an Entity-Relationship diagram a relationship is a significant real world association between entities. In the relational database model a relationship is the association between two or more tables in the database.

Repeating group A group of attributes or columns in a single entity or table that contains the same data item. For example, an order table that contains multiple columns to hold the order items.

Requirements definition The process of identifying and recording what data needs to be stored in a database and what processing needs to be done on that data.

Restore The process of returning a database to a useable state by retrieving a back-up from removable media.

Row A single entry in a table. Each row in a table describes a single instance of the thing about which the table is used to hold data.

Self-join A view or query in which a table is joined to itself. For example an employee table may contain a Foreign key that holds the identifier for a manager employee record. To show the details of the employee as well as his or her manager, the table needs to be joined to itself.

Server See Database server, File server.

Software A set of instructions that tell a computer what to do. This includes the operating system (such as Windows 95) and application programs (such as Microsoft Word or Access).

Sorting Placing the rows in a table in a specific order according to the values held in one or more columns. Sorting changes the logical order of the records – it does not change the physical order of the records stored in the tables concerned.

Storage device A piece of hardware used to store data in a computer system. Examples of storage devices include hard disks, floppy disks, tape drives, CD-ROM and so on.

Structured Query Language (SQL) A programming language used to define objects in a database and to retrieve and manipulate the data held in a relational database. International standards organisations have produced definitions of the language and most relational database systems provide a dialect of the language for database operations.

Sub-type In an Entity-Relationship diagram an entity may be split into two or more mutually exclusive sub-types.

Synonym Two different names that are used to refer to the same thing. For example, one department might call the number used to identify an employee the Staff number while another department might call the same number an Employee ID.

System software Computer programs that are used to control the physical components of the computer and to provide services to other programs.

Programs that control particular components, such as a printer or a hard disk are often known as 'device drivers'. The set of system software that controls the overall operation of the computer is called the 'operating system'. A Database Management System will use the file processing services of the operating system to physically record data in the files that make up the database.

Table The data in a database represented as and arranged as rows and columns. Tables are the logical structures that make up the definition of a database. The physical representation of the data (for example the contents of the files that make up the database) may be quite different.

Transaction A unit of work that must be completed as a whole or must fail completely. For example, when money is posted from one account to another in an accounting system there should be a debit to one account and a corresponding credit to another account. If one of these postings is allowed to be completed while the other fails, the integrity of the system is compromised.

Tuple Technical term for a single row in a table.

Union A relational database operation that creates a view that consists of all the rows in one table with all the rows in one or more other tables. By default duplicate rows are excluded, but it is possible to specify that all rows should be returned. Unlike queries involving joins that return a single row for each matching row in the tables, a union will return a row for every (unique) row in each table.

Unique identifier In an Entity-Relationship diagram the unique identifier is any attribute, or combination of attributes, that can serve, in all cases, to uniquely identify an instance of an entity. In the relational database model the unique identifier is any column, or columns, in a table that can be used to retrieve a single row in the table (see Primary key).

View A view can be used to display data from more than one table, to restrict the columns that can be seen, or restrict the rows that can be seen based on data values. Views are often referred to as virtual tables – they look and behave like tables, but are not defined as tables in the database. A view in Microsoft Access is known as a query.

Index